The Federal Loyalty-Security Program

D1564399

The Federal Loyalty-Security Program
The Need for Reform

Guenter Lewy

American Enterprise Institute for Public Policy Research
Washington and London

Guenter Lewy is professor of political science at the University of Massachusetts, Amherst, and a former visiting scholar at the American Enterprise Institute. He is the author of five books, including *America in Vietnam*.

Library of Congress Cataloging in Publication Data

Lewy, Guenter, 1923-
    The federal loyalty-security program.

    (AEI studies ; 378)
    Includes bibliographical references.
    1. Loyalty-security program, 1947-
I. Title. II. Series.
JK734.L48   1983   353.001'3242   83-2711
ISBN 0-8447-3518-3

AEI Studies 378

Printed in the United States of America

The First Amendment . . . requires that one be permitted to believe what he will. . . . It does not require that he be permitted to be the keeper of the arsenal.

Chief Justice Vinson,
American Communications Association v. *Douds*

Contents

Preface

This monograph draws attention to certain legal and political problems that have developed in the federal loyalty-security program during the last ten to fifteen years and have created serious difficulties for its effective functioning. My argument is that certain key provisions of the present personnel security program, now almost thirty years old, are badly outdated. They sweep too broadly, and at the same time they no longer adequately safeguard the loyalty and trustworthiness of officials in truly sensitive positions. I therefore recommend that the government abandon the pretense of an all-encompassing loyalty program and limit screening measures to positions that involve access to classified information or an ability to make or influence policy.

The Eisenhower loyalty-security program of 1953, under which we are still operating, was developed in response to security threats from the radical Left. Given the affinity of many segments of the Left for the Soviet Union, Cuba, and other so-called socialist countries in the third world, it is the Left rather than the militant Right that continues to constitute the more serious security problem. There is little danger that a member of the Ku Klux Klan will seek to promote the interests of the Communist powers, currently our most prominent adversaries. Most of my discussion here therefore focuses on the Old and the New Left, even though some of my remarks may have a wider application. I should also point out that this study does not aim to be a comprehensive examination of all aspects of the current personnel security program. Important issues such as the procedural rights of individuals affected by the loyalty-security program are discussed here only in passing and will be examined more fully in a larger work that is under way.

I want to express my gratitude to the many government officials who have aided me in the preparation of this study. I did not seek from them classified information, and none was disclosed to me. Most of them, however, preferred to talk on a "not for attribution" basis, and I honor this request by thanking them in this general way and without listing them by name. I am also indebted to colleagues and friends who have given me the benefit of their criticism. They, too, shall remain unnamed and thus will be spared responsibility for conclusions they may not agree with. Last but not least, I want to thank the Carthage Foundation for financial aid and the American Enterprise Institute for extending to me its hospitality during the academic year 1981–1982. Both of these supports were essential for the successful completion of this study.

1
Introduction: The Need for a Loyalty-Security Program

On March 25, 1980, Deputy Associate Attorney General William Robie told a congressional committee looking into the need to update the federal personnel security program, still formally based on President Eisenhower's Executive Order (EO) 10450 of 1953: "We feel that it is fair to say that the loyalty provisions of the security program established by the order are in complete disarray at the present time."[1] Anyone familiar with the current state of the federal loyalty-security program will have to agree with this appraisal. It is not the purpose of this monograph to sow panic or to suggest that the federal government today is honeycombed with subversives or that security officials are "soft" on Communism. The facts that made the Justice Department speak of a situation of "complete disarray," however, deserve to be more widely known. A few examples:

- Mere membership in the Communist party is not a disqualification for employment by the federal government, even for sensitive positions.
- Since 1977, the Office of Personnel Management (OPM), formerly the Civil Service Commission (CSC), no longer asks applicants for federal jobs, including critical-sensitive positions, to answer questions on application forms about past or present membership in the Communist party or other organizations seeking the violent overthrow of the government. These questions have been held to have a chilling effect on the First Amendment right of association.
- OPM has abolished the collection and maintenance of information on various extremist groups since this allegedly would amount to maintaining records on how individuals exercise their First Amendment rights. Such record keeping is held prohibited by the Privacy Act of 1974.

1. U.S. Congress, House, Subcommittee on Investigations of the Committee on Post Office and Civil Service, *Hearings on Federal Personnel Security Background Investigations,* 96th Cong., 2d sess., March 25, 1980, p. 3.

• Since 1968, no person has been denied employment or been dismissed from the federal government specifically on grounds of disloyalty or as a security risk. (There have been denials and dismissals for providing false answers to questions on application forms used before 1977 pertaining to membership in the Communist party.)

There are many different reasons for this state of affairs. Undoubtedly, the political climate of our day has contributed significantly to the almost complete abandonment of any loyalty yardstick in the personnel security program. Back in 1951, Professor Walter Gellhorn, a noted authority on administrative law at Columbia University Law School, expressed his understanding of the real dangers posed by Communist subversion and an aggressive Soviet Union: "But when all this has been fully acknowledged, one has still to ask whether the people of the United States have perhaps yielded to an overexcitement that will debilitate them if not soon controlled."[2] As it turned out, the American people overcame the exaggerated zeal in the hunt for subversives that often characterized the 1950s. Indeed, today, thirty years later, we may well face the opposite problem. If during the years of McCarthyism, all too many Americans suspected a Communist under every bed, the conviction now appears to be equally widespread that there are no Communists under any bed. For many people any attempt to focus attention upon weaknesses in our domestic security posture is tantamount to rekindling the hysteria and paranoia of the McCarthy era.

Perhaps the greatest damage that Senator Joseph McCarthy has caused this nation is that he succeeded in casting doubt upon the need for a serious and responsible concern with Communism and domestic security. His excesses have discredited the cause of anti-Communism; yet while the junior senator from Wisconsin in his day did indeed engage in something akin to "witch-hunting," use of this term is not really appropriate. Witches never existed; Soviet agents did and do.[3] Cord Meyer, a man who despite his high CIA position became a temporary casualty of the spirit of hysteria and political timidity then abroad in the land, has correctly noted that McCarthy "would never have achieved his national prominence unless there had in fact been serious Communist penetration and evidence available to the public of the government's failure to cope with it."[4]

2. Walter Gellhorn, ed., *The States and Subversion* (Ithaca, N.Y.: Cornell University Press, 1952), p. 359.

3. James Rorty and Moshe Decter, *McCarthy and the Communists* (Boston: Beacon Press, 1954), p. 5, n. 3.

4. Cord Meyer, *Facing Reality: From World Federalism to the CIA* (New York: Harper and Row, 1980), p. 81.

During the 1930s and 1940s, Communist activity in Washington was indeed substantial. Documentary evidence as well as the testimony of former Communist agents such as Elizabeth Bentley and Whittaker Chambers confirmed the fact of Communist penetration of practically every important government department during those years. Among the best known of these men were Alger Hiss, assistant secretary of state for international organization affairs; Larry Duggan, head of the State Department's Latin American desk; Lauchlin Currie, administrative assistant to President Roosevelt; and Frank Coe, top Treasury official, later to become head of the International Monetary Fund. In all, at one time there may have been as many as seventy-five persons employed by the federal government who were involved in Soviet espionage. Some of them were dedicated Communists, aware and proud of the fact that they were working for the Soviet Union; others were fellow travelers or were enmeshed in the various spy rings for a great variety of personal reasons. They helped each other to obtain jobs in specific agencies or to transfer to more strategic posts. They stole documents and, when possible, strove to influence government policy in a pro-Soviet direction. They were tolerated by superiors who, in the face of derogatory information supplied by the FBI, gave them the benefit of the doubt, or they slipped through security procedures that were lax and inefficient.[5]

In February 1945, the government found more than one thousand classified documents, some of them TOP SECRET, taken from the files of the Office of Strategic Services (OSS) and the War, Navy, and State departments, in the New York office of the left-wing magazine *Amerasia*. In June 1946, after the defection of the Russian embassy clerk Igor Gouzenko, the Canadian government published a report of a Royal Commission that revealed the existence of a far-flung espionage ring of Canadian citizens, some of them with links to the United States. Meanwhile, Elizabeth Bentley and Whittaker Chambers had told the FBI their stories of espionage within the federal government. At the same time, the cold war, triggered by the Soviet Union's designs on Greece and Turkey, was becoming a fact of political life. It was the cumulative effect of these disturbing events that led Congress to grant the right of summary dismissal to the heads of several agencies and that made President Truman, following the recommendations of the House Civil Service Committee, appoint the President's Temporary

5. The literature on this subject is extensive. See especially Earl Latham, *The Communist Conspiracy in Washington: From the New Deal to McCarthy* (Cambridge, Mass.: Harvard University Press, 1966); David J. Dallin, *Soviet Espionage* (New Haven, Conn.: Yale University Press, 1955); Herbert L. Packer, *Ex-Communist Witnesses: Four Studies in Fact Finding* (Stanford, Calif.: Stanford University Press, 1962); Allen Weinstein, *Perjury: The Hiss-Chambers Case* (New York: Alfred A. Knopf, 1978).

Commission on Employee Security, on November 25, 1946. The commission's report was released by the president on March 2, 1947. Three weeks later, attempting to head off more extreme demands made by several committees of Congress, President Truman issued EO 9835, "Prescribing Procedures for the Administration of an Employee Loyalty Program in the Executive Branch of the Government."[6]

The Truman loyalty program was not the first such screening procedure. Loyalty-security regulations had been introduced during the Revolutionary War and the Civil War. Early in World War I, President Wilson issued a confidential executive order authorizing the heads of departments and agencies to remove any employee when the retention of such employee "would be inimical to the public welfare by reason of his conduct, sympathies, or utterances, or because of other reasons growing out of the war. Such removal may be made without other formality than that the reasons shall be made a matter of confidential record, subject, however, to inspection by the Civil Service Commission."[7] On August 2, 1939, Congress enacted Section 9-A of the Hatch Act, which forbade federal employees to belong to an organization that advocated the overthrow of the country's constitutional form of government.[8] In 1942, the CSC issued a war regulation that broadened its power of dismissal and disqualified an applicant when the commission felt "a reasonable doubt as to his loyalty to the government of the United States."[9] But President Truman's program was the first systematic and all-inclusive screening program of federal employees.

The Truman loyalty program was in effect for six years. During this time, 4,756,705 loyalty forms on individuals, incumbents and applicants, were checked against the files of the FBI and other records and sources. In the cases of 26,236 persons, where questions of loyalty had been raised, the FBI conducted an investigation. Of these, 16,503 persons were cleared, including 252 on appeal; 6,828 left the civil service or withdrew their applications (1,192 after they had been sent interrogatories or charges); and 560 persons were removed or denied employment on grounds related to loyalty. (In the cases of 569 persons, the Department of the Army acted under security laws; 1,776

6. Executive Order 9835 of March 21, 1947, 16 F.R. 3690. For the more complete story of the genesis of the Truman program, see Eleanor Bontecou, *The Federal Loyalty-Security Program* (Ithaca, N.Y.: Cornell University Press, 1953), chap. 1.

7. Cited by Harold M. Hyman, *To Try Men's Souls: Loyalty Tests in American History* (Berkeley, Calif.: University of California Press, 1959), pp. 268-69.

8. 53 Stat. 1148, 5 U.S.C. 118j.

9. Sec. 18.2(c)(7), September 26, 1942, 5 C.F.R. Cum. Supp. 18.2(c)(7).

cases were incomplete when the program terminated.)[10]

On April 27, 1953, President Eisenhower established a new program in his EO 10450, which has continued in force to this day.[11] The Eisenhower program is entitled "Security Requirements for Government Employees," and the governing standard for clearance stresses security—employment and retention in employment are to be "clearly consistent with the interests of the national security" (section 2). The differences between the two programs, however, are relatively insignificant and bear mostly on matters of procedure. As before, government employees must be "of complete and unswerving loyalty to the United States" (Preamble), and many of the criteria for security clearance bear directly on matters of loyalty. Not every person who is a security risk is also disloyal. The employment in sensitive positions of individuals who drink to excess or take drugs or who are subject to pressure on account of relatives behind the Iron Curtain or who can be blackmailed because of their sexual orientation may present unacceptable risks to the national security, but such persons should not be branded disloyal. Nonetheless, a person who is disloyal because of his allegiance to another country or to an ideology profoundly at odds with fundamental American values is also a security risk. In these cases, the categories of loyalty and security overlap, and efforts aimed at screening out such individuals are therefore properly referred to as a loyalty-security program. Eisenhower's EO 10450, even though called a security program, is no less concerned with loyalty than its predecessors.

The numerical results of the Eisenhower program soon fell victim to partisan controversy as to whether Republicans or Democrats were tougher on disloyal government employees, a dispute that became known as the "numbers game." To this day, no comprehensive system exists for reporting the outcome of personnel investigations or for clearly distinguishing cases of loyalty from judgments made on traditional standards of suitability. During the first two years of the program, it appears, there were 315 dismissals involving doubt about loyalty.[12] Between 1956 and 1970, 522 applicants and 362 appointees, in the cases of whom loyalty questions had been raised, were made the subject of an FBI investigation. Only 12 applicants and 4 appointees were, however, rated out on the basis of reasonable doubt as to loy-

10. Civil Service Commission, *1953 Annual Report* (1954), p. 32, cited by Ralph S. Brown, Jr., *Loyalty and Security: Employment Tests in the United States* (New Haven, Conn.: Yale University Press, 1958), p. 55.

11. 18 F.R. 2489.

12. See Brown, *Loyalty and Security*, pp. 58-59.

alty. There have been no denials on the grounds of questionable loyalty or security since 1968.[13]

The argument is often heard today that the loyalty programs established after World War II were a complete failure because they did not detect any acts of disloyalty punishable by law. "At a cost to federal agencies from 1947 to 1957 of about $350 million," writes a recent critic, "the federal government was unable to uncover a single spy."[14] This objection misses the point, for these programs were designed not to catch the guilty but to exclude the potentially guilty. In view of the necessary shortcomings of a decent criminal law and of an imperfect counterespionage system, a free society must attempt to protect the integrity of its government by assessing the probability of future misbehavior, whether willing or unwilling, whether deliberate or through negligence or ignorance, on the part of those who occupy positions of trust and who could cause harm to the national interest. Unfortunately, few such situations allow for positive, conclusive evidence of future conduct.

The decision whether a person is worthy of trust is necessarily fraught with uncertainties, and untrustworthiness and unreliability can rarely be established beforehand as firmly as a court of law can deal with actions that have already taken place. The degree of risk deemed acceptable will vary with the nature and responsibility of the positions sought or held. Whether the standard employed is "reasonable doubt as to the loyalty of the person involved" or whether the requirement is that employment be "clearly consistent with the interests of the national security," the task of applying these criteria is inevitably colored by subjectivity. Taking into consideration prior experience with similar cases, frail men have to attempt to evaluate imperfect men.

In judging the success or failure of the effort to protect the government from disloyal persons, the number of individuals denied employment or dismissed is not decisive. If some of the individuals screened out—small as their total number may be—had the potential to cause serious damage to the nation's well-being, the maintenance of a clearance program would be justified. Moreover, public knowlege of the existence of an investigative process will itself act as a deterrent and will discourage those apprehensive of being found out. To be

13. Figures provided by Kimbell Johnson, director, Bureau of Personnel Investigations, Civil Service Commission, for U.S. Congress, House, Committee on Internal Security, *Report on the Federal Civilian Employee Loyalty Program*, 92d Cong., 2d sess., January 3, 1973, p. 52.

14. Robert J. Goldstein, *Political Repression in Modern America* (Boston: G. K. Hall, 1979), p. 374.

sure, an appraisal of the worth of such programs must take account not only of benefits but also of costs and unintended consequences. There is general agreement, for example, that President Truman's loyalty program exacted a heavy price in its negative effects upon the morale and caliber of the civil service. A sober and experienced observer noted in 1952:

> It is clear that the emphasis that has been placed upon loyalty and orthodoxy among public employees has served to encourage mediocrity in the public service. Federal workers have learned that it is wise to think no unusual thoughts, read no unusual books, join no unusual organizations, and have no unusual friends. What this has cost the government in terms of loss of independence, courage, initiative, and imagination on the part of its employees is impossible to say, but it is clear that the cost has been great.[15]

The lesson to be learned from this experience is not that the government can do without a loyalty program. The possibility that badly conceived or incompetently administered efforts to safeguard vital security interests may jeopardize civil liberties is not a conclusive argument against such efforts. Similarly, the suggestion that loyalty tests have never provided security and that real security "has emerged from within, from strengths garnered by lives and sacrifices freely offered"[16] is probably no more than half-truth. We are living in a dangerous world, and the problems posed by espionage, infiltration, and subversion are not figments of a paranoid imagination.

Acts of disloyalty and espionage on the part of civilian government workers and military personnel continue to occur at a steady pace. The positions of these men have often been minor, but the damage caused by their activities has been no less serious. In 1961, Irvin Chambers Scarbeck, second secretary of the U.S. embassy in Warsaw, was sentenced to thirty years on a charge of espionage. In 1963, Nelson C. Drummond, a navy enlisted man, was sentenced to life imprisonment on a similar charge, and two more espionage cases involving military personnel occurred in 1965 and 1967. Edwin Gibbons Moore II, a retired CIA employee, was sentenced to life imprisonment on a charge of espionage in June 1977; the same year Christopher John Boyce, a TRW worker employed by the CIA, was given a sentence of forty years for passing sensitive data on reconnaissance satellites to the Russians. In 1978, William Kampiles, a CIA

15. Robert K. Carr, *The House Committee on Un-American Activities* (Ithaca, N.Y.: Cornell University Press, 1952), pp. 456-57.

16. Hyman, *Men's Souls*, p. 345.

employee, was sentenced to forty years in prison for selling a manual on another satellite to Soviet agents. Also in 1978, Ronald L. Humphrey, an employee of the United States Information Agency, was convicted of espionage for passing government documents to the Vietnamese in France. In January 1981, a former CIA employee, David H. Barnett, received a sentence of eighteen years for selling sensitive information to the Russians. In October 1981, Joseph George Helmich, Jr., a former army code custodian, was sentenced to life in prison for selling top secret information about a coding machine. This list of treachery is not exhaustive. It does not include the numerous cases of industrial espionage that have occurred. Also, there were those who got away, such as two employees of the highly sensitive National Security Agency, Vernon F. Mitchell and William H. Martin, who defected to the Soviet Union in 1960.[17]

It is often said that today's Soviet agents do their dirty work for money rather than for ideological reasons and that a loyalty program therefore would not be able to screen out or apprehend such individuals. There is truth in this argument; most of the instances of espionage that have been discovered indeed appear to have taken place for financial reasons. And yet, human motives are usually complex and often composed of several elements. For example, in the recent case of Lt. Christopher M. Cooke, deputy commander of a Titan missile site in Kansas, who was arrested in May 1981 and admitted giving the Russians secret missile data, it is impossible to tell whether this air force officer was simply naive in his announced intention of gaining the good will of the Soviets in order to prod them into disarmament or whether he also had other, less beneficent aims. Moreover, in the case of at least one of these men, Christopher John Boyce, the dominant motive was indeed ideological. Since Boyce's way of thinking is widespread among many people, both young and old, who were radicalized by the events of the 1960s, it deserves some attention.

Born in 1953, Boyce attended high school and college in California during the time of an unpopular war, easy availability of drugs, and widespread disenchantment with patriotism. Eventually Boyce's estrangement from American society reached such intensity that he was ready to betray secrets to the Russians. He had not intended to serve the interests of the Soviet Union, he wrote in a letter from prison after his conviction, but had wanted to commit "an act of defiance" against a corrupt and cancerous system. The foundations of this country were a sham; industrialism and technology were dragging humanity to-

17. For some of the information in this paragraph I am indebted to David Martin's "The Erosion of the Federal Employee Security Program: A Critique," unpublished manuscript, December 1981.

ward collapse. The superpowers had accumulated thousands of nuclear weapons, which they were prepared to unleash upon each other. Eventually, he hoped, a new global society would emerge devoid of competing militarisms; "the new treason is the rejection of nationalistic society and its exploitive and butchering adjuncts."[18]

We do not know how many other persons who think like Boyce want to work or presently do work for the government of the United States. Still less can we predict how many of these individuals will decide to take the fateful step of committing espionage. Anyone who has had contact, however, with the generation that matured in the 1960s knows that Boyce's deep sense of alienation from American society is not an unusual occurrence in this group. This country today has many thousands of "Boyces" and consequently a large number of potential spies. Assuming that the protection of national security is a valid concern, it would therefore be the height of irresponsibility to forgo the use of protective measures aimed at preventing persons of this mentality from reaching positions of trust and responsibility. To discover the "Boyce" syndrome in applicants for sensitive positions requires a personal interview conducted by well-trained investigators knowledgeable in politics and psychology. The crucial importance of creating such a staff of highly qualified investigators will be discussed in a subsequent chapter.

In addition to confused young people like Christopher Boyce, we also have to reckon with the far smaller number of activists who belong to the New Left. This is an ever-changing scene of numerous, loosely organized groups that share a critical view of both the United States and the Soviet Union and whose sympathies lie with various national liberation movements in the third world. The great majority of these people will never consider working for the Soviets; yet from the point of view of the Russians they are probably a good recruiting ground. The New Left shares the Communists' animus toward American capitalism, yet its members are known as anti-Communists, and they will therefore encounter few difficulties in entering government service. The New Left is critical of bureaucratic Communism, but it is pleased with the assistance the Soviet Union provides for various revolutionary movements. New Leftists therefore will tend to support many Russian policies in the developing world. The New Left played a prominent part in the antiwar movement during the Vietnam conflict; many of its constituent groups not only, or primarily, sought peace in Vietnam, but openly or surreptitiously worked for a victory of the Vietnamese Communists and a defeat of the United States. The New

18. Quoted in Robert Lindsey, *The Falcon and the Snowman: A True Story of Friendship and Espionage* (New York: Pocket Books, 1980), p. 433.

9

Left can be expected to adopt a similar stance with regard to any future conflict in the third world in which the United States may become involved.

In a free society, the New Left has a right to criticize a foreign policy that it regards as exploitative and imperialistic, yet one may question the suitability of such people for important and sensitive government positions. Just as one would not consider a member of the pacifist American Friends Service Committee a suitable candidate for a position involving the preparation of war plans in the Defense Department, so one may doubt the fitness of individuals adhering to the world outlook of, say, the Institute for Policy Studies for sensitive positions involving the formulation or implementation of U.S. foreign or military policy. It is to be hoped that even a Democratic administration, committed to a more benevolent policy toward the third world than is practiced by the Reagan administration, would hesitate to entrust its fortunes to men like Marcus G. Raskin, Arthur Waskow, Richard J. Barnet, or Ralph L. Stavins, who are on record, at one time or another, as praising the Communist regimes of Vietnam, Cambodia, and Cuba and who consider the United States a repressive society that must be radically restructured. There is a real question whether such men would be willing conscientiously to carry out policies they strongly oppose on political and moral grounds. Given their distrust of authority, their selective acceptance of "bourgeois legality," their disdain for mere "formal" democracy, and their romanticizing of the individual conscience, would they be willing to follow the directions and orders of their bureaucratic superiors, or would they insist on interposing their personal moral judgments whenever they felt strongly enough about the issue in contention? These questions deserve to be raised and answered in a calm and deliberate manner. Personnel decisions on both the "Boyces" of this country and members of the New Left will undoubtedly have to be made on a case-by-case basis, yet one must at least be aware of the difficulties that may arise in connection with such applicants.

There are also some segments of the Old Left about which one may wish to raise questions of loyalty. Numerically, these groups are insignificant, yet their announced aims dictate caution. The Maoist Progressive Labor Party, for example, has repeatedly called upon its members to join the military services in order to build there a revolutionary base.

> The proletariat's chance of overthrowing the bourgeoisie and smashing the bourgeois state in the event of an immediate revolutionary situation depends in great measure on the degree of disaffection within the bosses' armed forces. . . .

> Loyalty to the U.S. means loyalty to the bosses' state. . . . We
> should reserve our bullets for the brass and their ruling-class
> masters.[19]

It may well be that this kind of revolutionary rhetoric will be regarded by the courts as protected by the First Amendment, yet even "mere membership" in such an organization should probably be grounds for some very thorough probing. The same goes for the Trotskyist Spartacist League and its youth arm, both of which have expressed their sympathy for the Weather Underground, believe in the unconditional defense of the Soviet Union against "imperialistic attack," and have hailed the Russian occupation of Afghanistan.[20]

The radical scene today is different from that of several decades ago when the main concern of both Congress and the law enforcement agencies was with forceful overthrow of the government or outright spying in the service of the Soviet Union. The mainline Communist parties and the New Left go out of their way to disavow both of these aims and often indeed are committed to neither. There is evidence to indicate that Soviet intelligence no longer uses Communist parties for the recruitment of espionage agents. Altogether, it has become more difficult than in the past to decide who is to be regarded as a foreign agent. What of someone, James Q. Wilson has asked,

> who travels to a foreign country to receive training, or who
> accepts foreign money to cover the expenses of his organiza-
> tion, or who secretly collaborates, without pay, with foreign
> powers in the pursuit of their policy objectives? At the ex-
> tremes, the distinctions are easy to make, but in the middle,
> where several American dissident groups may well belong,
> the distinctions will be maddeningly difficult.[21]

One is reminded here of Humbert Wolfe's ditty about the British journalist:

> You cannot hope to bribe or twist,
> Thank God! the British journalist.
> But seeing what the man will do
> Unbribed, there's no occasion to.

The old problems of disloyalty and subversion, then, have not

---

19. "Soldiers and Sailors—A Key Force for Revolution," *PL* (Summer-Fall 1981), pp. 12, 19-20.

20. *Workers Vanguard*, no. 287 (August 14, 1981), p. 12. See also Anna Quindlen, "Around Columbia, Protest and Apathy," *New York Times*, October 28, 1981.

21. James Q. Wilson, "Buggings, Break-Ins and the FBI," *Commentary* (June 1978), p. 57.

disappeared, but what do these words mean in the world of the 1980s? Clarity of these terms is essential for recognizing the problems we face today, yet in fact one finds here a great deal of intellectual confusion.

Loyalty, most would agree, relates to certain qualities of the heart, mind, and character. We say that someone is loyal to his friends when he supports them in good and in bad times, and the same dedication can be observed in persons who are committed to the political institutions and liberties of their country and are prepared to make great sacrifices to defend them. Conversely, a disloyal person is one who does not reciprocate the kindness and help his friends have extended to him and who deserts them in the hour of need. In the political context of a democratic society, a disloyal individual is one who fails to acknowledge the benefits he has enjoyed as a result of living under a constitutional form of government, based on the rule of law, and who is unwilling to defend the democratic institutions of his country against its enemies. (A conscientious objector to war presumably would make his contribution to the common defense in the form of some alternative service.) When such a person substitutes for loyalty to his own country and its traditions and values superior loyalty to another state, committed to destroying the democratic way of life, the pattern of disloyalty is manifest.

It is possible, however, for a person to be disloyal without actively serving the interests of another country. An individual who, while enjoying the benefits of our Bill of Rights, is committed to the destruction of the democratic form of government and its system of ordered liberty is disloyal irrespective of whether he also helps the foreign enemies of this country. Similarly, it is possible to be disloyal without running afoul of the law. Those who seek to bring down the democratic system by unconstitutional means, that is, by force and violence, act illegally in addition to being disloyal. But persons who want to abolish the constitutional foundations of our society by legal means and substitute for them a totalitarian scheme of government or a racist dictatorship are no less disloyal to the heritage of this country than those who work for the violent overthrow of the government. The fact that they may be legally entitled to adhere to their antidemocratic ideals and goals does not absolve them of disloyalty.

The same principles hold for subversion. Literally, to subvert means to turn from beneath. In the political context of our time, subversives are those who seek to undermine the democratic institutions of our society without openly acknowledging this aim. Communist parties, in particular, have perfected the tactics of subterfuge and deception by hiding their real goals behind phraseology and slogans designed to appeal to the gullible; Communists profess to seek the triumph of democracy and the liberation of the oppressed. They also create organizations that front for the Communist party—so-called Communist front organizations that serve the interests of the party under the guise of some honorable activity, such as promoting racial harmony or world peace. Communists often attempt to infiltrate and take over mass organizations, such as trade unions, and use them for their political purposes.

Such subversive activity is not necessarily illegal. To be politically dishonest or to plant disinformation is not to act criminally. Yet such conduct undermines the democratic process by creating distrust; it corrupts the marketplace of ideas by concealing the true sponsors and beneficiaries of certain policies or organizational schemes. Similarly, subversive activities need not necessarily be instigated by foreign governments or foreign organizations, though in fact they often are. The serious damage Communist front organizations can cause American foreign policy was highlighted in a recent State Department Special Report that described the effect of such groups in connection with the planned modernization of NATO theater nuclear weapons, the development of the neutron bomb, and the leftist insurgency in El Salvador.[22] Obviously, many, perhaps most, efforts to oppose current U.S. policy on these issues have nothing to do with Communist machinations, but propaganda campaigns in which avowed objectives are cloaks for the interests of a foreign power or for plans to destroy democratic institutions should be given the only name appropriate—subversion.

As a result of a series of court rulings (which will be examined in a later chapter), federal officials, anxious to avoid charges of McCarthyism, in recent years have all but abandoned disloyalty as grounds for disqualification from public employment. Government officials entrusted with the enforcement of the loyalty-security program (EO 10450) openly acknowledge that they no longer know what meaning to give to terms like "disloyalty" and "subversion." When CSC Chairman Alan K. Campbell was asked in the course of a congressional hearing in 1978 whether the commission had criteria "as to what kind of affiliations and what kind of activity constitutes proper cause for believing that the applicant in question may not be loyal to the United States, or may be committed to the subversion of the U.S. Government," he replied: "No, sir, we do not."[23] And in 1980, the director of

22. U.S. Department of State, *Soviet "Active Measures": Forgery, Disinformation, Political Operations*, Special Report no. 88 (October 1981).

23. U.S. Congress, Senate, Subcommittee on Criminal Laws and Procedures of the Committee on the Judiciary, *Hearings on the Erosion of Law Enforcement Intelligence and Its Impact on the Public Security*, part 4, 95th Cong., 2d sess., 1978, p. 215.

OPM's Division of Personnel Investigations, Peter Garcia, noted the absence of any criteria that could be used in a definition of loyalty, and he called upon Congress to provide the necessary guidance.[24] Members of Congress, in turn, have expressed their shock that the executive branch no longer seems to know what constitutes loyalty to this country.

The term "subversion," too, has lost its traditional meaning, and for some it is no longer acceptable altogether. After the disclosure of various improper activities on the part of the intelligence services, the Senate Select Committee to Study Governmental Operations with Regard to Intelligence Activities—the Church committee—in 1976 called for abandoning the term "subversion."[25] The same year, Attorney General Edward H. Levi limited the domestic intelligence function of the FBI to activities that involve a violation of federal law, such as overthrowing the government or depriving persons of their rights under the Constitution. Applying the same logic and intent upon living down a reputation for having an overly broad concern with the politics of its personnel, the Department of Defense (DOD) now takes the position that in "the context of DOD investigative policy, subversion refers only to such conduct as is forbidden by the laws of the United States."[26] The net effect of all this has been to limit the investigation of disloyal and subversive conduct to activities that are also illegal, a narrowing of concern that, as I have suggested earlier, is decidedly inappropriate. The purpose of a loyalty-security program, we should again remind ourselves, is not to detect or punish crimes but to provide the government with reliable and trustworthy personnel and to keep potential spies or subversives out of sensitive positions.

It is arguable that loyalty is irrelevant for most government positions, since they involve neither access to classified information nor an ability to make or influence policy. This pragmatic argument, involving the question of the scope of the loyalty-security program, will receive the careful attention it deserves in the concluding chapter of this study. This is not, however, the problem confronting us at present. Today disloyalty and subversion not only are ignored in connection with nonsensitive positions but, with the exception of the intelligence agencies, for all practical purposes are being disregarded

24. House, Subcommittee on Investigations of the Committee on Post Office and Civil Service, *Hearings on Personnel Security*, p. 38.

25. U.S. Congress, Senate, Select Committee to Study Governmental Operations with Regard to Intelligence Activities, *Final Report*, 94th Cong., 2d sess., 1976, p. 176.

26. U.S. Department of Defense, *Personnel Security Program*, DOD 5200.2-R (December 1979), 2-401, p. II-8.

altogether. Disqualification is possible only for activities that are also illegal. Membership in Communist or subversive organizations (in the old-fashioned sense of that term) is not a bar to employment even in sensitive positions unless a person has the specific intent to promote the unlawful aims of the group to which he belongs. One would not insist that it is necessary to catch a judge who is an active and dedicated member of the Ku Klux Klan in the act of announcing his intent to discriminate against blacks and Jews before concluding that he is unfit for judicial office. Yet this is the yardstick now being used to measure disloyalty and subversion.

Organizing and implementing a loyalty-security program that is effective yet not oppressive is not an easy task. It requires finding a satisfactory balance between the demands of national security and the interests of individual freedom. The personnel security programs in place today provide the individual government worker or applicant for a government job far greater protection against arbitrary treatment than was the case in the 1940s and 1950s. Indeed, many feel that we have gone too far and have extended procedural safeguards to the point of impairing efficiency and the ability to dismiss the unsuitable. To detail the problems created in this area of civil service law and practice would require another book. It is the political components, however, that have forced the loyalty-security program badly out of balance.

"Must a government of necessity be too *strong* for the liberties of its own people, or too *weak* to maintain its own existence?" Abraham Lincoln asked in 1861.[27] The answer to this question should be that we need not choose between protecting the government against the disloyal and sacrificing our freedoms. Loyalty and security in government service can be protected within the framework of traditional principles of justice and fairness. As the Supreme Court reminded us not very long ago, "unless Government safeguards its own capacity to function and to preserve the security of its people, society itself could become so disordered that all rights and liberties would be endangered."[28] The government has the duty to protect itself against those who would subvert it, for "while the Constitution protects against invasions of individual rights, it is not a suicide pact."[29]

27. Special Session Message, July 4, 1861, cited by William J. Donovan and Mary Gardiner Jones, "Program for a Democratic Counter Attack to Communist Penetration of Government Services," *Yale Law Journal*, vol. 58 (1949), p. 1211.

28. U.S. v. U.S. District Court, 407 U.S. 297, 312 (1972).

29. Kennedy v. Mendoza-Martinez, 372 U.S. 144, 160 (1963).

2

Overview of the Current Program

The present personnel security program is based on Executive Order (EO) 10450, promulgated by President Eisenhower in 1953. The regulations issued by the various federal departments and agencies, which implement this basic charter, are broadly similar both in the substantive criteria applied and in the investigative and adjudicative procedures used. Another common denominator is that since 1968 no department or agency has invoked the authority of EO 10450 to remove an employee on grounds of security or questionable loyalty.

In accordance with EO 10450, Section 3(a), all appointments to civilian positions in the federal government require a National Agency Check (NAC), which includes a check of the fingerprint and investigative files of the FBI (for persons with prior military service, also a check of military records) as well as written inquiries to appropriate local law enforcement agencies, former employers and supervisors, references, and schools attended. For aliens or naturalized citizens it includes a check of the records of the Immigration and Naturalization Service. This basic investigative procedure is known as the National Agency Check with Inquiries (NACI); it is handled by the Office of Personnel Management (OPM) for all federal agencies. (Under the Civil Service Reform Act of 1978, OPM is the successor agency to the Civil Service Commission—CSC.) If the NACI finds adverse information, the investigation can be expanded to resolve questions about the candidate's suitability. Cases where a person may be subject to coercion by a foreign power or where there is a question of possible disloyalty must be referred to the FBI for a full field investigation.[1]

A full field investigation initially was required for positions designated by the head of a department or agency as sensitive by virtue of the material adverse effect on the national security that an occupant of such a position could cause. Since 1965, sensitive positions have been divided into noncritical-sensitive and critical-sensitive positions. Applicants for and appointees to the former now ordinarily receive only

1. Sec. 8(d) of EO 10450, 18 F.R. 2489; *Federal Personnel Manual (FPM)*, chap. 736: "Investigations," 1-7(a).

an NACI, though the head of an agency can initiate a full field investigation when he considers it appropriate. Applicants and appointees to critical-sensitive positions receive a full field investigation, which, in addition to the NAC, includes personal interviews conducted by an investigator with present and former employers, supervisors, fellow workers, references, neighbors, and school officials.[2] Generally, these investigations cover the most recent five years of a person's background and activities, or since the eighteenth birthday, whichever is the shorter period. OPM conducts full field investigations for about fifty-five federal agencies. Background investigations for the Department of Defense (DOD) are conducted by the Defense Investigative Service. The Department of State and the intelligence agencies run their own investigations. The FBI conducts the more important investigations for the Department of Justice.

The largest single employer of civilian personnel in the federal government is the Department of Defense. About 75 percent of all sensitive positions in the civilian sector of the government are in the DOD. In addition to almost 1 million civilian employees, DOD also has under its administrative roof about 2 million military personnel. Since 1979, DOD has had a personnel security program that consolidates in a single program and under one set of rules procedures for both civilian and military personnel.[3] DOD also conducts the Industrial Security Program, which screens access to classified information for some 11,000 industrial contractors with a total of more than 1 million employees.[4]

Except where delegated to agencies by special agreement, OPM determines the suitability of most applicants in the competitive civil service. Determinations of suitability for applicants to critical-sensitive positions and decisions on appointments are made by the employing agencies on the basis of information supplied by OPM's Division of Personnel Investigations. Adjudications in the Department of Defense are handled by adjudicative facilities in components such as the army, air force, and navy. The State Department has its own applicant review panel, and so do the intelligence agencies. In the case of practically all positions in the competitive service, adverse personnel decisions can be appealed to the Merit Systems Protection Board (established by the Civil Service Reform Act of 1978 and fulfilling the appeals

2. *FPM*, chap. 736, subchap. 2.

3. U. S. Department of Defense, *Personnel Security Program*, DOD 5200.2-R (December 1979).

4. The industrial personnel security program is based on EO 10865, February 20, 1960, 25 F.R. 1583, *Safeguarding Classified Information within Industry*. The implementing regulation is DOD 5200.6, reissued most recently on December 20, 1976.

functions of the former CSC) and ultimately to the courts.

EO 10450 (as amended most recently by EO 11785 of 1974) requires that all persons "employed in the departments and agencies of the Government, shall be reliable . . . and of complete and unswerving loyalty to the United States" (Preamble) and that the employment of all persons be "clearly consistent with the interests of the national security" (Section 2). Whether a person conforms to this standard is dependent upon the development of information related to the following criteria enumerated in Section 8(a):

(1) Depending on the relation of the Government employment to the national security:

(i) Any behavior, activities, or associations which tend to show that the individual is not reliable or trustworthy.

(ii) Any deliberate misrepresentations, falsifications, or omissions of material facts.

(iii) Any criminal, infamous, dishonest, immoral, or notoriously disgraceful conduct, habitual use of intoxicants to excess, drug addiction, or sexual perversion.

(iv) Any illness, including any mental condition, of a nature which in the opinion of competent medical authority may cause significant defect in the judgment or reliability of the employee, with due regard to the transient or continuing effect of the illness and the medical findings in such case.

(v) Any facts which furnish reason to believe that the individual may be subjected to coercion, influence, or pressure which may cause him to act contrary to the best interests of the national security.

(2) Commission of any act of sabotage, espionage, treason, or sedition, or attempts thereat or preparation therefor, or conspiring with, or aiding or abetting, another to commit or attempt to commit any act of sabotage, espionage, treason or sedition.

(3) Establishing or continuing a sympathetic association with a saboteur, spy, traitor, seditionist, anarchist, or revolutionist, or with an espionage or other secret agent or representative of a foreign nation, or any representative of a foreign nation whose interests may be inimical to the interests of the United States, or with any person who advocates the use of force or violence to overthrow the government of the United States or the alteration of the form of government of the United States by unconstitutional means.

(4) Advocacy of use of force or violence to overthrow the government of the United States, or of the alteration of the form of government of the United States by unconstitutional means.

(5) Knowing membership with the specific intent of further-

18

ing the aims of, or adherence to and active participation in, any foreign or domestic organization, association, movement, group, or combination of persons (hereinafter referred to as organizations) which unlawfully advocates or practices the commission of acts of force or violence to prevent others from exercising their rights under the Constitution or laws of the United States or of any State, or which seeks to overthrow the Government of the United States or any State or subdivision thereof by unlawful means.

(6) Intentional, unauthorized disclosure to any person of security information, or of other information disclosure of which is prohibited by law, or willful violation or disregard of security regulations.

(7) Performing or attempting to perform his duties, or otherwise acting, so as to serve the interests of another government in preference to the interests of the United States.

(8) Refusal by the individual, upon the ground of constitutional privilege against self-incrimination, to testify before a congressional committee regarding charges of his alleged disloyalty or other misconduct.

EO 10450, Section 1, had extended the summary suspension and unreviewable dismissal power in national security cases, given to the heads of eleven departments and agencies by Public Law 81-733 of August 26, 1950,[5] to all departments and agencies of the federal government. In 1956, the Supreme Court in the case of *Cole* v. *Young* ruled this extension invalid on the grounds that the summary procedures authorized by Public Law 81-733 were meant to apply only to positions directly affecting the national safety and security.[6] The effect of this decision has been to limit the removal procedures of EO 10450 to applicants and employees who occupy sensitive positions, but in practice, and for a variety of reasons discussed later in this chapter, agencies have stopped using the removal authority of Public Law 81-733 and EO 10450 for any adverse action whatever. Between 1956 and 1968, there were sixteen denials of employment and removals on the grounds of security and questionable loyalty; there have been none since 1968.[7] During the following years all denials and removals have been on the basis of suitability criteria under regular civil service procedures.

5. 64 Stat. 476, 5 U.S.C. 7532.

6. 351 U.S. 536 (1956).

7. Testimony of Robert J. Drummond, director, Bureau of Personnel Investigations, Civil Service Commission, February 2, 1978, before U.S. Congress, Senate, Subcommittee on Criminal Laws and Procedures of the Committee on the Judiciary, *Hearings on the Erosion of Law Enforcement Intelligence and Its Impact on the Public Security,* part 4, 95th Cong., 2d sess., 1978, p. 217.

Since the enactment of the Civil Service Act of 1883, the Civil Service Commission has had the authority to investigate the ability and fitness of applicants to the federal civil service. Under this grant of authority and several subsequent laws and executive orders, OPM and the various departments and agencies today determine the suitability of applicants and employees. They can deny an appointment or remove an employee if and when it has been determined that such action will "promote the efficiency of the service."[8] Among the reasons that may be considered a basis for disqualification are the following:

(1) Delinquency or misconduct in prior employment;
(2) Criminal, dishonest, infamous or notoriously disgraceful conduct;
(3) Intentional false statement or deception or fraud in examination or appointment;
(4) Refusal to furnish testimony as required by §5.4 of this chapter;
(5) Habitual use of intoxicating beverages to excess;
(6) Abuse of narcotics, drugs, or other controlled substances;
(7) Reasonable doubt as to the loyalty of the person involved to the Government of the United States; or
(8) Any statutory disqualification which makes the individual unfit for service.[9]

It will be noted that the eight criteria of suitability above include loyalty to the government of the United States. This criterion (7) was inserted by the CSC into the Civil Service War Regulations of September 26, 1942, and has been there ever since.[10] Yet, again, practice tends to differ from written regulations. Just as no department or agency since 1968 has made use of any of the eight criteria of EO 10450, Section 8(a), listed above, no denials or removals since that time (if not longer) have been based on the civil service criterion of disloyalty. As required by Section 8(d) of EO 10450 and applicable civil service regulations, cases where a person is thought to be subject to pressure to act contrary to the interests of national security or to be disloyal to the United States are still referred to the FBI. Nonetheless, not only has the number of such referrals declined drastically—from 191 in fiscal year 1973 to 5 in fiscal year 1981—but none of these referrals has

8. Cf. 5 U.S.C. 3301ff.
9. 5 C.F.R. 731.202(b).
10. Sec. 18.2(c)(7). Cf. Eleanor Bontecou, *The Federal Loyalty-Security Program* (Ithaca, N.Y.: Cornell University Press, 1953), p. 14.

resulted in a denial or removal on grounds of disloyalty.[11] An undeterminable number of individuals have been denied appointment or have been removed for violating such other criteria of suitability as intentionally making a false statement on application forms or being unreliable and untrustworthy on account of past conduct. But disloyalty as such is no longer used as a disqualification.

The reasons for these developments, here summarily stated, are these:

1. A string of Supreme Court decisions has narrowed the grounds on which a person's affiliation with subversive organizations can be used as a disqualification for the federal service, while the requirements of due process of law in personnel actions have been made very stringent.

2. Under these circumstances, to substantiate subversive associations or conduct may risk the exposure of FBI informants who could be required to give evidence as witnesses. In 1965, CSC Chairman John W. Macy therefore informed the heads of all departments and agencies that before issuing charges under EO 10450 the Department of Justice should be consulted. "That Department is in the best position to advise agencies whether the proposed charges are fully supported, and the extent to which confrontation and cross-examination of witnesses will be required." This requirement for consultation with the Department of Justice is now part of the civil service rules.[12] As we have seen, no charges using EO 10450 have been pressed since 1968.

3. Because of the constitutional problems often raised by security and loyalty cases and because suitability criteria cover much the same ground in different language, the tempting thing has been to ignore the former and to use the latter. As CSC General Counsel Anthony L. Mondello put it in congressional testimony in 1972, "it is usually easier to prove the existence of these other grounds than it is to prove a want of security or reasonable doubt as to loyalty."[13]

4. In view of the controversies surrounding the loyalty-security

11. In addition to the 191 cases referred, the bureau opened another 1,200 cases on its own on the basis of information revealed in the NAC. Since 1977, the FBI no longer initiates such investigations. (Information supplied by Loyalty and Applicants Section, Criminal Investigative Division, Federal Bureau of Investigation).

12. *FPM*, chap. 732: "Personnel Security Program," 1-6(b); Macy's letter of November 18, 1965, is reproduced in U.S. Congress, House, Committee on Internal Security, *Hearings Regarding the Administration of the Subversive Activities Control Act of 1950 and the Federal Civilian Employee Loyalty-Security Program*, part 2, 91st-92d Cong., 1971, pp. 595-97.

13. House, Committee on Internal Security, *Hearings Regarding the Subversive Activities Control Act*, part 4, 1972, p. 5884.

program of the 1950s, there has been a reluctance to stigmatize individuals with the label of security risk or disloyalty.

5. Section 12 of EO 10450 requested the Justice Department to continue to develop a list of foreign or domestic organizations that the attorney general, after appropriate investigation and determination, had designated as totalitarian, Fascist, Communist, or subversive—a practice begun under the Truman loyalty program.[14] Under this authority, Attorney General Herbert Brownell furnished the heads of departments and agencies with a list of organizations for which membership in or affiliation with was to be considered by the departments and agencies as one factor in connection with employment or retention of individuals in the federal civil service. This so-called list of subversive organizations led an uneasy existence, involving several reorganizations and court challenges, and was finally abolished by President Nixon's EO 11785 of June 4, 1974.[15] Since then, federal agencies and OPM have been without central guidance as to the kinds of organizational affiliations that are to be considered an indication of possible disloyalty and thus potentially disqualifying. Similarly, the FBI, apart from espionage, sabotage, links to a foreign power, or outright acts of violence, is today without guidance as to the type of conduct that would warrant investigation of an individual's loyalty.

6. A series of federal court decisions has led to the elimination of questions dealing with membership in the Communist party and other subversive organizations on forms used by OPM to screen applicants for federal employment. The ability of investigators to probe for such information orally is likewise circumscribed; OPM has also abandoned any record keeping on subversive organizations or individuals affiliated with them. DOD continues to make use of questions dealing with organizational affiliations in its screening for sensitive positions.

7. Last but not least, one must mention the political climate of the 1960s and 1970s, in which anti-Communism was often regarded as a manifestation of McCarthyism and paranoid hysteria. As a result of the abuses of the Watergate scandal, the very concern with national security is seen by many as suspect. It is probably significant in this connection that whereas President Ford's executive order of 1976 "United States Foreign Intelligence Activities" retained the FBI's traditional assignment to "detect and prevent espionage, sabotage, *subversion*, and other unlawful activities by or on behalf of foreign powers"[16]

14. Part 3, paragraph 3, of EO 9835, March 21, 1947, 12 F.R. 1935.
15. 39 F.R. 20053.
16. Sec. 4(g)(1) of EO 11905, February 18, 1976, 41 F.R. 7703.

(italics added), any reference to subversion was missing from the corresponding executive orders issued by Presidents Carter and Reagan.[17] The very term "subversion," it would appear, can no longer be used without raising the specter of witch hunts and unacceptable inroads upon civil liberties.

In the chapters that follow, these developments will be discussed in more detail.

17. EO 12036 of January 24, 1978, 43 F.R. 3674; EO 12333 of December 4, 1981, 46 F.R. 59941.

3

The Effect of Court Decisions

The Significance of Organizational Ties

In 1892, Oliver Wendell Holmes laid down what for a long time served as the controlling view on the question of the citizen's claim to a government job. "The petitioner may have a constitutional right to talk politics, but he has no constitutional right to be a policeman."[1] Government employment was seen as a privilege and not a right; the citizen had to take such employment on the terms offered to him.

In the years since World War II this doctrine has slowly been laid to rest. In *Adler* v. *Board of Education*, a case involving New York state teachers, the U.S. Supreme Court in 1952 repeated Holmes's dictum that teachers had no right to work in the state school system on their own terms, but the Court added that the terms laid down by the state authorities had to be reasonable.[2] "We need not pause to consider whether an abstract right to public employment exists," said the Court in *Wieman* v. *Updegraff*, a case involving an Oklahoma loyalty oath for state officers and employees decided in the same year. "It is sufficient to say that constitutional protection does extend to the public servant whose exclusion pursuant to a statute is patently arbitrary or discriminatory."[3] Due process of law was violated when a state found persons disloyal solely on the basis of organizational membership, regardless of their knowledge of the aims of the organization to which they belonged. Disqualification from government service on the basis of mere association with a proscribed organization, thus lumping together innocent with knowing membership, violated the due process clause of the Fourteenth Amendment as an assertion of arbitrary power.

In 1966, fourteen years later, the Court took another step in narrowing the grounds on which a potentially disloyal person could be kept out of or removed from a government job. At issue was an

1. McAuliffe v. Mayor of New Bedford, 155 Mass. 216, 220, 29 N.E. 517 (1892).
2. Adler v. Board of Education, 342 U.S. 485 (1952).
3. Wieman v. Updegraff, 344 U.S. 183, 192 (1952).

Arizona statute that imposed criminal penalties and discharge upon state employees who took an oath of loyalty while at the same time they knowingly and willfully retained membership in the Communist party or any other organization that aimed at the violent overthrow of the government of the state. The U.S. Supreme Court in *Elfbrandt* v. *Russell* struck down this law as violating the freedom of association protected by the First Amendment, applicable to the states through the Fourteenth Amendment. A statute touching protected rights and liberties, said the Court, had to be narrowly drawn. Many of those who join an organization do not share its unlawful purposes or participate in its unlawful activities; it therefore was not permissible to penalize mere membership in the Communist party or its subordinate organizations, even with knowledge of the unlawful purposes of these groups. "A law which applies to membership without the 'specific intent' to further the illegal aims of the organization infringes unnecessarily on protected freedoms. It rests on the doctrine of 'guilt by association' which has no place here."[4] The same principle was enunciated a year later in *Keyishian* v. *Board of Regents,* which involved university teachers at a state institution in New York and which overruled the *Adler* decision of 1952. "Mere knowing membership without a specific intent to further the unlawful aims of an organization is not a constitutionally adequate basis for exclusion from such positions as those held by appellants."[5]

In both the *Elfbrandt* and the *Keyishian* cases, four justices dissented from this holding. The Court majority, they argued, appeared to apply the same standard to public employment that the Court had developed with regard to direct governmental interference with private citizens' First Amendment rights, specifically in connection with the Smith Act's prohibition of the advocacy of violent overthrow of the government.[6] In *Scales* v. *United States* the membership clause of the Smith Act had been held to "reach only 'active' members having also a guilty knowledge and intent" to further the illegal ends of the organization, accompanied by significant action in its criminal enterprise.[7] But the issue of what kind of revolutionary advocacy the government could tolerate, argued the four justices, should not control the question of the employability of knowing members of the Communist party. "They [these cases] did not suggest that the state or federal government should be prohibited from taking elementary precautions against its employees forming knowing and deliberate affiliations with

4. Elfbrandt v. Russell, 384 U.S. 11, 19 (1966).
5. Keyishian v. Board of Regents, 385 U.S. 589, 606 (1967).
6. Title I of the Alien Registration Act of 1940, 54 Stat. 670, 18 U.S.C. 2385.
7. Scales v. United States, 367 U.S. 203, 228 (1961).

those organizations who conspire to destroy the government by violent means."[8]

Justice White, the author of this dissent, returned to the same point a year later in *United States* v. *Robel*, decided in 1967, when he dissented from a decision of the Court invalidating the exclusion of Communists from employment in industrial defense facilities as provided by the Subversive Activities Control Act of 1950.[9] Congress, White argued, should be entitled to take suitable precautionary measures to protect defense plants of critical importance to the security of the country. "Some Party members may be no threat at all, but many of them undoubtedly are, and it is exceedingly difficult to identify those in advance of the very events which Congress seeks to avoid."[10] Restrictions on the political activities of government employees or workers in defense plants, the dissenters insisted, should not be treated in the same way or judged by the same standards as criminal statutes affecting First Amendment rights of the American people. The risk to the national security created by disloyal persons in sensitive positions was necessarily much greater than the danger resulting from the unhindered advocacy of revolution among the public at large.

In effect, then, the Court majority appears to have concluded that public employees cannot be disqualified for associational activities that cannot also be punished criminally. The Court has reached this decision despite the fact that Congress and the Supreme Court itself have repeatedly gone on record as finding that the Communist party cannot be considered an ordinary political party and that membership in this and similar organizations therefore has to be assessed differently from political activity in the ranks of the Republican or Democratic party. Congress stressed this point in enacting legislation such as the Alien Registration Act of 1940 and the Internal Security Act of 1950. It is reasonable to conclude, stated Justice Jackson in 1950, that behind its political party façade the Communist party actually is a conspiratorial organization, controlled by a foreign power, that the party therefore "is something different in fact from any other substantial party we have known, and hence may constitutionally be treated as something different in law."[11]

This finding appears to have been put aside by a majority of the Warren Court in the 1960s, and in response to this change the govern-

8. Justice White (joined by Justices Clark, Harlan, and Stewart) dissenting in Elfbrandt v. Russell, 384 U.S. 11, 22 (1966).

9. Title I of the Internal Security Act of 1950, 64 Stat. 987, 50 U.S.C. 781. The section voided was 5(a)(1)D.

10. United States v. Robel, 389 U.S. 258, 287 (1967).

11. American Communications Association v. Douds, 339 U.S. 382, 423 (1950).

ment has adjusted the loyalty-security program to the "guilty knowledge and intent" test. EO 11785, issued by President Nixon on June 4, 1974, changed the membership criterion of EO 10450, Section 8(a)(5), from "membership in, or affiliation or sympathetic association with" a Fascist, Communist, or subversive organization to "knowing membership with the specific intent to furthering the aims of" organizations unlawfully advocating or practicing the commission of acts of force or violence.[12] This change has laid down a criminal yardstick for disqualification from public employment that is decidedly inappropriate for a personnel security program. As Justice Vinson said so well in *American Communications Association* v. *Douds,* in 1950, "the First Amendment . . . requires that one be permitted to believe what he will. . . . It does not require that he be permitted to be the keeper of the arsenal."[13]

Another group of cases reflecting a similar trend concerns the questions about membership in the Communist party on civil service application forms. A federal district court in *Stewart* v. *Washington,* decided in 1969, struck down a federal loyalty oath as an unconstitutional violation of First Amendment freedoms. Under a law enacted in 1955, an individual who accepted office or employment in the government of the United States had to execute an affidavit that he did not advocate "the overthrow of our constitutional form of government" and that he was not "a member of an organization that he knows advocates the overthrow of our constitutional form of government."[14] This affidavit, said the court, was excessively broad and vague because it applied to all positions, whether sensitive or custodial, and because it did not limit itself to overthrow by force and violence. Moreover, it reached mere passive members of such organizations who might not have an evil intent to take unlawful actions.[15] The Justice Department decided not to appeal this decision, and the affidavit is no longer in use. The decision presumably does not affect the disqualification of persons advocating overthrow of the government from public employment required by the same statute.

In a related series of decisions, the courts invalidated questions dealing with organizational affiliations. In *Soltar* v. *Postmaster General,* a federal district court in 1967 upheld the refusal of an applicant for a postal job to answer questions about past or present membership in the Communist party and other organizations seeking the violent overthrow of the government. These questions at that time were part

12. Sec. 3 of EO 11785, June 4, 1974, 39 F.R. 110.

13. American Communications Association v. Douds, 339 U.S. 382, 412 (1950).

14. Public Law 84-330 of August 9, 1955, ch. 690, 69 Stat. 624-625, 5 U.S.C. 3333 and 7311.

15. Stewart v. Washington, 301 F. Supp. 610, 612 (1969).

of the standard employment application forms.[16] "By probing into protected as well as unprotected areas involving speech and associations," the court found, "these questions have a 'chilling effect' on the exercise of First Amendment rights in that persons who desire federal employment will 'think first' before joining any political organization."[17]

In *Zuckerman* v. *United States,* another district court ruled in 1971 that the government had no legitimate interest in ascertaining the associations and political beliefs of a resident physician in a Veterans Administration hospital. Since under applicable Supreme Court rulings the holder of a nonsensitive position could not be dismissed merely because he associated with Communists or subversive groups, he could not be dismissed for refusing to answer questions about such associations.[18] The same conclusion was reached in *Cummings* v. *Hampton,* decided the same year and upheld by a Court of Appeals in 1973, in another case involving physicians serving a temporary appointment in a VA hospital. The court distinguished the case at hand from cases involving admission to the bar. In that context, such questions had been upheld by the Supreme Court on the grounds that states had a right to insist on having lawyers who, as officers of the court, were dedicated to law and the peaceful and reasoned settlement of disputes.[19] The court decided, however, no comparable government interest that might outweigh "the chilling effect on the exercise of First Amendment rights" existed in the case of medical interns.[20]

Again, the Justice Department decided not to appeal these cases, and the Civil Service Commission eventually eliminated the membership questions from its standard application form for nonsensitive positions. In 1977, going a step further, the CSC decided to omit these questions from the corresponding form for sensitive positions as well on the grounds that these questions had a "chilling effect on the First Amendment right of association" and were unconstitutionally vague.[21] "Useful information can be gained through other investigative means. Furthermore, these questions are primarily used to impeach persons who falsely answered the questions in the negative or

16. Questions 27 and 28 on SF-171.
17. Soltar v. Postmaster General, 277 F. Supp. 579, 580 (1967).
18. Zuckerman v. United States, 329 F. Supp. 957 (1971).
19. Konigsberg v. State Bar, 366 U.S. 36 (1961); Law Students Civil Rights Research Council v. Wadmond, 401 U.S. 154 (1971).
20. Cummings v. Hampton, 485 F. 2d 1153, 1155 (1973).
21. Questions 21-24 on SF-86.

to dissuade persons from applying who believe their backgrounds might raise suspicions."[22]

The elimination of the loyalty questions from the application forms for sensitive positions did not meet the approval of the Department of Defense. "It is difficult to conceive processing an applicant/nominee for a sensitive position, whether it concerns straight access to classified information or assignment to more sensitive duties such as in the National Security Agency or presidential support activity areas," argued the director of DOD's Security Plans and Programs, "without posing questions related to unconstitutional activities." We do not believe "that the courts ever intended to preclude the asking of questions, in connection with assignment to sensitive duties, relating to membership in and support of organizations which advocate acts of force or violence or which seek to overthrow the government of the United States by unlawful means."[23] To this day, therefore, the Defense Department continues to use the membership questions abandoned by the Civil Service Commission.

There is judicial precedent and support for the Defense Department's position in this matter. Past or present membership in the Communist party, the Supreme Court ruled in 1951, is a fact public employees may have to disclose to their employer, for it "may prove relevant to their fitness and suitability for the public service. Past conduct may well relate to present fitness; past loyalty may have a reasonable relationship to present and future trust. Both are commonly inquired into in determining fitness for both high and low in private employment."[24] Public employees owed their government "frankness, candor and cooperation" when examined as to their fitness.[25] Membership in the Communist party as such was not necessarily grounds for automatic disqualification, a federal court of appeals decided in 1962 in *Ogden* v. *United States,* a case involving the Industrial Security Program. The determination, however, "whether an individual may be trusted with classified defense material carries with it authority to ask him, at the threshold of the inquiry, about his relationship if any with the Communist party." At the very least, disclosure of such membership could provide a significant investigatory lead. "The

22. H. Patrick Swygert, general counsel, CSC, to Deane C. Siemer, general counsel, DOD, December 9, 1977.

23. Daniel J. Dinan, acting director, Security Plans and Programs, DOD, to Robert Gilliat, Office of the General Counsel, DOD, December 15, 1977.

24. Garner v. Board of Public Works, 341 U.S. 716, 720 (1951).

25. Beilan v. Board of Public Education, 357 U.S. 399, 405 (1958).

relevance of the inquiry to the protection of a vital national interest is plain. The restriction upon freedom of association is limited."[26] The existence of a "chilling effect" upon First Amendment rights, the Supreme Court ruled in *Younger* v. *Harris* in 1971, "has never been considered a sufficient basis, in and of itself, for prohibiting state action."[27] If the effect of inhibiting First Amendment freedoms was minor and incidental to a substantial governmental interest, then the restriction of such freedoms was defensible.[28] "The vague words 'chilling effect' cover many degrees of chill," noted Judge Gesell of the D.C. District Court in 1972, "and it is necessary to distinguish between the fear of catching flu, a possible shiver or two, and that hard chill that stifles free exercise of a definite constitutional right."[29]

The courts thus have repeatedly affirmed the right of the government to seek information "reasonably necessary for a rational judgment to be reached with respect to security clearance"[30] and "to deny employment to individuals who refuse to answer questions relevant to fitness or suitability for public service."[31] Such questions, as the Supreme Court insisted in *Sheldon* v. *Tucker*, decided in 1960, cannot include the listing of "every conceivable kind of associational tie—social, professional, political, avocational, or religious"; many of these relationships could have no possible bearing upon an employee's "competence or fitness."[32] At the same time, and certainly as far as screening for sensitive positions is concerned, the government's right to seek *relevant* information about an applicant's reliability and loyalty would seem to be firmly established.

Could the government obtain this kind of information by means other than asking questions about political associations on application forms? This issue is important because one of the requirements the Supreme Court has laid down for tolerating an incidental restriction of First Amendment rights is "the lack of alternative means" for furthering the valid and substantial governmental interest at stake.[33] In the case of the written loyalty questions, to invoke this test does not lead to an easy and straight answer.

It is difficult to satisfy the "lack of alternative means" criterion if that test is interpreted narrowly and literally. It is probably possible to

26. Ogden v. United States, 303 F. 2d 724, 731 (1962).
27. Younger v. Harris, 401 U.S. 37, 51 (1971).
28. United States v. O'Brien, 391 U.S. 367, 377 (1968).
29. American Servicemen's Union v. Mitchell, 54 F.R.D. 14, 18 (1972).
30. Gayer v. Schlesinger, 490 F. 2d 740, 754 (1973).
31. Richardson v. Hampton, 345 F. Supp. 600, 608 (1972).
32. Shelton v. Tucker, 364 U.S. 479, 488 (1960).
33. Younger v. Harris, 401 U.S. 37, 51 (1971).

run an effective security program without such written questions as long as government investigators make it a practice to ask questions about potentially disqualifying associations during the personal interviews conducted as part of a full field investigation. This was the position of the CSC when it abolished the use of these questions on application forms for sensitive positions in 1977, and OPM investigators are indeed authorized to make inquiries about an individual's associations in the case of "associations that deny another person's rights under the constitution . . . associations that advocate the overthrow of legally constituted units of government by violent means . . . associations that engage in the commission of crimes against persons or property."[34] Similar provisions govern the personnel investigations of the Defense Investigative Service (DIS). Investigators should

> determine if subject and/or the immediate family has, or formerly had membership in, affiliation with, sympathetic association towards, participated in, or subscribed to or regularly read publications of any foreign or domestic organization, association, movement, group, or combination of persons which unlawfully advocates or practices the commission of acts of force or violence to prevent others from exercising their rights under the Constitution or laws of the United States or of any state, or which seeks to overthrow the Government of the United States or any state or subdivision thereof by unlawful means (hereinafter referred to as subversive). Emphasis will be placed on determining the individual's knowing membership with the specific intent of furthering the aims of, or adherence to and active participation in, any of these activities described above.[35]

DOD officials, who argue the importance of the written questions, stress that such questions provide important investigative leads, which facilitate the investigator's task and help him establish or refute "knowing membership" and "specific intent" on the part of the individual. The forms put applicants on notice that all answers given by them on the application forms are subject to investigation and that a false or dishonest answer may be grounds for disqualification or dismissal and, under Section 1001 of Title 18 of the U.S. Code, may be punishable by fine or imprisonment. These sanctions may deter some

---

34. Office of Personnel Management, *Conducting and Reporting Personnel Investigations: Investigator's Handbook*, FPM Supplement (Internal) 736-71 (July 1, 1981), pp. VI-13–VI-14.

35. Defense Investigative Service, *Manual for Personnel Security Investigations*, DISM 20-1 (January 30, 1981), pp. 3-20.

potentially disloyal persons from applying and may make some applicants more honest than they otherwise might be. Whether these advantages would be sufficient to overcome the "lack of alternative means" test is an open question that so far has not been tested in the courts.

There is also the question how often individuals with subversive ties will volunteer this information on application forms. The main advantage of asking these written questions, as the CSC had argued in 1977, would indeed appear to be the easier possibility of removing persons subsequently found to have falsified their answers. It is simpler to establish that an individual made a false statement concerning his affiliation with a subversive organization than it is to prove knowing membership with intent to advance the illegal aims of such an organization.

The most important issue raised by the questions on political ties is probably not whether they should be asked on the application forms or orally by field investigators, but rather what kind of information the government should seek in loyalty-security investigations. Because the Supreme Court majority has laid down the same rule for disqualification from public employment that the Court has developed for squaring the First Amendment with punishment for advocacy of violent overthrow and membership in an organization that advocates revolution—the "guilty knowledge and intent" test—government lawyers have used the same criterion when they phrased questions about organizational associations. This practice appears to involve a basic confusion. Even if one holds the government's right to disqualify applicants for employment to the same stringent standard that the courts have insisted on with regard to a criminal statute limiting First Amendment rights, this standard does not have to govern the kinds of questions asked of applicants or nominees to sensitive positions. The information about organizational ties sought by way of these questions does not lead to automatic disqualification, but is merely one of several factors to be weighed in determining overall fitness for a position of importance to the nation's security and well-being. In such cases to limit the inquiry to questions that will reveal ties to organizations engaged in criminal activity, such as the use of force to deprive citizens of their rights under the Constitution or the violent overthrow of the government, is not really sufficient for establishing either fitness or loyalty. There are many organizations that stay clear of any outright criminal conduct, but that, nevertheless, harbor subversive designs or serve the interests of foreign powers. Membership in such organizations should be known to security adjudicators, whatever the use they make of this information.

Last, there is one other unnecessary legal complication that may arise when questions used in a personnel security investigation are linked too closely to the "guilty knowledge and intent" test. An individual asked whether he has knowing membership in a Communist organization, accompanied by a specific intent to further the illegal aims of this group, may well be entitled to invoke the protection of the Fifth Amendment against compulsory self-incrimination. Indeed, the Supreme Court has ruled that even mere association with the Communist party presents sufficient risk of prosecution to support a claim of privilege against self-incrimination.[36] The completion of the application forms is a voluntary act, but a person who does not provide all the information sought is not given full consideration, and the processing of his application often effectively ends. Answers elicited upon threat of the loss of employment, the courts have held, are compelled answers.[37] In order to prevent a possible Fifth Amendment challenge, a person asked questions of the kind now used in some security clearance proceedings may therefore have to be granted immunity from criminal prosecution. Since, in many instances, the government may want to preserve the right to bring criminal charges at some future time, the use of the "guilty knowledge and intent" test in loyalty questions may thus be inadvisable on still another ground.

Even when the government has obtained information on organizational ties and other matters bearing on an applicant's loyalty, the Privacy Act of 1974 may prevent it from being included in an applicant's file. Section (e)(7) of the Privacy Act forbids the keeping of records that describe how individuals exercise rights guaranteed by the First Amendment unless authorized by statute or by the individual concerned or as part of an authorized law enforcement activity.[38] In the case of *Gann* v. *United States Civil Service Commission*, a federal court ruled in 1977 that personnel security investigations are not an authorized law enforcement activity and that the CSC therefore was not entitled to maintain in its files information on plaintiff's membership in left-wing organizations, his alleged "leftist" political views, his religion, or his conscientious objector status. It might be admissible, said the court, to include the fact of membership in groups advocating the overthrow of the government because such membership by law is a disqualification for public employment.[39] Neither that statute nor the

36. Albertson and Proctor v. Subversive Activities Control Board, 382 U.S. 70 (1965).

37. Cf. most recently Lefkowitz v. Turley, 414 U.S. 70 (1973).

38. Public Law 93-579, of December 31, 1974, 88 Stat. 1896, 5 U.S.C. 552a(e)(7).

39. The court had in mind here Public Law 84-330 of August 9, 1955, 69 Stat. 624, 5 U.S.C. 7311, which codified the Hatch Act and made unnecessary appropriations riders to the same effect that had been in use since 1941.

Privacy Act, however, permitted "wholesale maintenance of all materials relating to political beliefs, associations, and religion."[40]

In addition to a violation of Section (e)(7) of the Privacy Act, the court also found an infringement of Section (e)(6), which requires that, before dissemination, an agency make "reasonable efforts" to ensure that records about an individual are "accurate, complete, timely, and relevant for agency purposes." The investigative file in the case at hand had been compiled during the years 1942–1947, when the plaintiff had been an employee of the federal government. To make this thirty-year-old file available to the Library of Congress, where the plaintiff had applied for employment in 1975, the court ruled, "without deleting the obviously untimely and irrelevant information contained therein," represented a clear violation of the intent of the law.

The *Gann* decision is not necessarily absolutely dispositive of these issues. Nevertheless, as the CSC told the General Accounting Office in 1978, the decision "has undoubtedly resulted in a wariness on the part of agencies conducting security or suitability background investigations about collecting information that may conceivably be regarded as an exercise of First Amendment rights."[41] The CSC itself has cited the *Gann* decision as a reason for dismantling its security index, a subject discussed in the next chapter.

Issues of Due Process of Law

In addition to entertaining objections to the loyalty-security program on First Amendment grounds, the courts in recent years have also insisted on applying more stringent standards of procedural due process of law under the Fifth Amendment. The case law in this area is vast and cannot possibly be treated comprehensively here. Some of the high points, however, must be sketched out. Some of these decisions have added to the difficulties of the loyalty-security program.

In the benchmark case of *Bailey* v. *Richardson*, decided in 1950 and upholding a dismissal under the Truman loyalty program, the Court of Appeals of the District of Columbia held that public employment was a "privilege" and not a "right" and that procedural due process guarantees were therefore inapplicable.[42] In the ensuing years this

40. Gann v. United States Civil Service Commission, unreported memorandum opinion of May 10, 1977, Civil Action no. 76-1263. The opinion is reproduced in U.S. Congress, Senate, Subcommittee on Criminal Laws and Procedures of the Committee on the Judiciary, *Hearings on the Erosion of Law Enforcement Intelligence and Its Impact on the Public Security*, part 4, 95th Cong., 2d sess., 1978, pp. 233-36.

41. U.S. General Accounting Office, *Impact of the Freedom of Information and Privacy Acts on Law Enforcement Agencies*, GGD-78-108, November 15, 1978, p. 28.

42. Bailey v. Richardson, 182 F. 2d 46 (1950), affirmed without opinion by an equally divided Supreme Court, 341 U.S. 918 (1951).

holding has been thoroughly undermined. Constitutional rights, including those of procedural due process, the Supreme Court has held, no longer "turn upon whether a governmental benefit is characterized as a 'right' or as a 'privilege.'"[43] The precise meaning of "due process," however, is not easily captured by a formula. Due process embodies those rules of fairness that have evolved through centuries of Anglo-American constitutional history. "Its exact boundaries," stressed Chief Justice Warren in 1960, "are undefinable, and its content varies according to specific factual contexts."[44]

In line with this reasoning, the courts have tended to insist on higher standards of due process in security programs affecting the private sector. In *Parker* v. *Lester,* decided in 1955, a court of appeals held that the denial of security clearance to merchant seamen under the Coast Guard Port Security Program[45] without affording them the right to a hearing and to some confrontation and cross-examination of the witnesses who allegedly had furnished derogatory information violated the due process clause of the Fifth Amendment.[46] The court emphasized the special status of these seamen, whose private employers did not necessarily have any contractual relationship with the federal government: "The liberty to follow their chosen employment is no doubt a right more clearly entitled to constitutional protection than the right of a government employee to obtain or retain his job."[47]

Four years later, the Supreme Court applied the same principle to a case involving the industrial security program. In *Green* v. *McElroy* the Court held that, in the absence of explicit authorization from either the president or the Congress, the Defense Department could not deny a security clearance to an engineer in a private firm without providing him with the opportunity to confront and cross-examine individuals who had given evidence against him. These traditional rights of due process, said the Court, were especially important in this kind of proceeding "where the evidence consists of the testimony of individuals, whose memory might be faulty or who, in fact, might be perjurers, or persons motivated by malice, vindictiveness, intolerance, prejudice, or jealousy."[48] The Court seemingly retreated from this ruling in *Cafeteria Workers* v. *McElroy,* where it upheld the exclusion on security grounds of a short-order cook from the premises of a

43. Graham v. Richardson, 403 U.S. 365, 374 (1971).

44. Hannah v. Larche, 363 U.S. 420, 442 (1960).

45. The program is based on the so-called Magnuson Act of August 9, 1950, 64 Stat. 427, 50 U.S.C. 191, amending Title II of the Espionage Act of 1917. It was implemented by EO 10173, October 18, 1950, 15 F.R. 7005.

46. Parker v. Lester, 227 F. 2d 708 (1955).

47. Ibid., p. 717.

48. Greene v. McElroy, 360 U.S. 474, 496 (1959).

naval gun factory without affording her a hearing where she might have had the opportunity to refute the charges made against her.[49] This decision, however, stressed the traditionally great authority of navy commanding officers and relied heavily upon the fact that the employee had been offered work at other facilities and thus had not been deprived of employment opportunities.[50]

In cases involving government employees, due process at times has been given a somewhat narrower interpretation. In 1965 a court of appeals ruled that "an agency of the Federal government cannot, without permitting cross-examination and confrontation of adverse witnesses, take detrimental action against a person's substantial interest on loyalty or security grounds—unless, at the least, Congress (or the President, if he is the source of power) has expressly authorized the lesser procedure."[51] But in the case of a probationary employee of the navy, discharged for failing to disclose membership in an organization on the attorney general's list, the same court a year later refused to require the navy "to divulge the names of confidential informants and to place other confidential information at plaintiff's disposal."[52]

More recently, a federal district court in *Jane Doe* v. *United States Civil Service Commission* has ruled that "the right to confront and cross-examine witnesses applies to administrative proceedings where an interest protected by the Due Process Clause is at stake."[53] The decision continued the trend of providing hearing rights to individuals adversely affected by stigmatizing information collected by the government and, for the first time, extended this right to applicants for public employment. The ruling also, and again for the first time, made the personnel officials involved in the case liable for money damages.

In addition to the constitutional arguments relied upon by the court in the *Jane Doe* case, there is also the requirement of the Privacy Act of 1974 that agencies which maintain records on individuals must ensure the "accuracy" of these records.[54] According to *Jane Doe*, a person who challenges the accuracy of such records with significant and weighty countervailing evidence must be granted the opportunity to cross-examine the sources of the derogatory allegations included in an agency file. The ruling calls into question the right and ability of OPM to rely upon derogatory information concerning disputed facts provided by unidentified sources, and this raises the issue of how to

49. Cafeteria Workers v. McElroy, 367 U.S. 886 (1961).
50. This point was stressed in Kiiskila v. Nichols, 433 F. 2d 745, 747 n.2 (1970).
51. Garrott v. United States, 340 F. 2d 615, 618 (1965).
52. Bennett v. United States, 356 F. 2d 525, 529 (1966).
53. Jane Doe v. United States Civil Service Commission, 483 F. Supp. 539, 579 (1980).
54. 5 U.S.C. 552a(g)(1)(C).

strike a balance between the government's need for information and the interest of the individual charged with disloyalty to learn the identity of his accusers and to be able to cross-examine them.

It is known that much significant information from past associates and employers is obtained only on promises of confidentiality. An OPM study involving a random sample of 2,000 background investigations during July–August 1980 revealed that 5 percent of all sources had been granted confidentiality or informant status and that in 47 percent of these cases the granting of confidentiality had been essential to preserve all the meaningful information in the case.[55] Yet, given the importance of the right of confrontation to the achievement of fairness and justice in such proceedings, when an adverse personnel action is challenged, the government probably should be willing to waive the confidentiality at least of ordinary citizens who have provided information. Another possibility is to provide that when an adverse action is challenged in court, the government be required to go before the trial judge and, in an ex parte proceeding, justify the protection of the informant. The court in some situations might require the government to produce the informant in camera and make him testify under oath as to the validity of the information given.[56] Such a procedure would be especially important in the case of informants employed by the intelligence agencies, whose identity cannot be compromised without great cost. This or a similar system would be an important improvement upon the present practice of denying the right of confrontation in certain national security cases, even though appropriate consideration is to be given to the fact that the individual affected did not have the opportunity of cross-examination.[57]

The efficacy and rigor of personnel investigations will also be inhibited by the fear of individual liability on the part of officials. In a series of cases since the landmark decision of *Bivens* v. *Six Unknown Named Agents of the Bureau of Narcotics,* handed down by the Supreme Court in 1971,[58] the courts have held that the violation of a constitutional right by a federal agent acting under his authority gives rise to a federal cause of action for damages. As an increasing number of federal employees have been dragged through drawn-out and often frivolous lawsuits, and despite the small odds that an employee will

55. OPM, Division of Personnel Investigations, *Background Investigations: Statistical Analysis,* DPI-22, June 1981, p. 5.

56. This suggestion is made by Robert P. Dwoskin, *Rights of Public Employees* (Chicago: American Library Association, 1978), p. 76.

57. See, for example, EO 10865 of February 24, 1960, 25 F.R. 1583, Sec. 4.

58. Bivens v. Six Unknown Named Agents of the Bureau of Narcotics, 403 U.S. 388 (1971).

actually be held liable, morale within the civil service has suffered. In a dissenting opinion in one of these cases, four justices of the Supreme Court predicted that not only will the threat of litigation "inhibit officials from taking action which they should not take in any event. It is the cases in which the grounds for action are doubtful or in which the actor is timid, which will be affected by today's decision."[59] Because of the likely chilling effect on personnel investigations of the *Jane Doe* and earlier decisions, legislation has been introduced in the Congress that would free an investigator or adjudicator from liability as long as he acted in good faith in carrying out established policy or guidelines.

Another series of court decisions has narrowed the grounds upon which OPM or an agency may take action against an applicant or employee for off-duty conduct in order to promote the efficiency of the service. While at one time in such cases an agency had relatively unfettered discretion to decide what constituted adequate cause for removal or denial of appointment, since the decision of *Norton* v. *Macy* in 1969, the courts have adopted the so-called nexus theory. The sufficiency of the charges against the appellant, the court ruled in that case, "must be evaluated in terms of the effects on the efficiency of the service of what in particular he has done or has been shown to be likely to do."[60] In other words, agencies bear the burden of proof, substantiated by the administrative record, that a specific rational connection or nexus exists between the employee's off-duty conduct and (1) his ability to perform the duties and responsibilities of his position satisfactorily, or (2) the agency's ability to perform its mission without deleterious effects on the efficiency of the service in general.

Norton v. *Macy* involved the rights of a homosexual, but the nexus principle enunciated there has been held applicable to other kinds of off-duty conduct as well. A federal court, for example, ruled in 1971 that the secretary of health, education, and welfare had acted arbitrarily and capriciously when he denied a commission in the Public Health Service on security grounds because the applicant had voiced his opposition to the Vietnam War and because he had signed a petition favoring a memorial to Dr. W. E. B. Du Bois, a noted black educator who at an advanced age had become a member of the American Communist party. "The plaintiff has the right not to be disqualified from public employment solely because he exercised First Amendment rights."[61] There existed no nexus between these political activities and the requirements of this position in the Public Health Service.

59. Butz v. Economou, 438 U.S. 478, 527 (1978).
60. Norton v. Macy, 417 F. 2d 1161, 1166 (1969).
61. Kahn v. Secretary of Health, Education and Welfare, 53 F.R.D. 241, 246-47 (1971).

Similarly, in a case involving a civilian employee on a military base, who had been discharged for membership in a group opposed to the war in Vietnam, a court of appeals ruled not only that caustic and sharp attacks upon government officials or policy were not an adequate basis for disqualification from public employment but also that a free society had a special interest in encouraging such an uninhibited and robust debate on public policy.[62]

Yet some behavior may be regarded as so outrageous as to bring an agency of the government into ridicule or disrepute and thus undermine the public's confidence in its government. This was the ruling of a court of appeals in 1969 in the case of a civilian employee of the Department of the Army dismissed because of homosexual acts, some of them involving soldiers. "Any schoolboy knows that a homosexual act is immoral, indecent, lewd and obscene."[63] Such activities will affect the standing of the government in the eyes of the public and cannot be tolerated. It is not absurd to fear, added one of the judges concurring in upholding the dismissal, "that a public which loses respect for the employees of an agency will lose respect for the agency itself." The agency, therefore, had the right to require its employees to refrain from off-duty behavior that the public regarded as scandalous and disgraceful. The impairment of the reputation of the agency was the nexus between the conduct of the employee and the agency's ability to fulfill its mission without ill effects on the efficiency of the service in general.[64] Similarly, in 1975 the Court of Claims upheld the dismissal of an Internal Revenue Service employee who had intentionally overstated his tax deductions since "the IRS is rightly concerned with its image of honesty and integrity."[65]

The reasoning employed in this case resembles the opinion of Justice Frankfurter in a loyalty oath case decided in 1951. The state, argued Frankfurter in *Garner* v. *Board of Public Works*, has a right to assure itself "of fidelity to the very presuppositions of our scheme of government on the part of those who seek to serve it." In the context of our time, he went on to say, membership in the Communist party is relevant not only to effective and dependable government but also "to the confidence of the electorate in its government."[66] Whether either homosexuality per se or "mere membership" in the Communist party on the part of public employees today would still be seen as undermin-

62. Kiiskila v. Nichols, 433 F. 2d 745 (1970).
63. Schlegel v. United States, 416 F. 2d 1372, 1378 (1969).
64. Ibid., p. 1383.
65. Hoover v. United States, 513 F. 2d 603, 606 (1975).
66. Garner v. Board of Public Works, 341 U.S. 716, 725 (1951).

ing the confidence of the people in their government and thus establish grounds for dismissal is questionable.

There is another way in which homosexuality and membership in certain political organizations could establish a nexus leading to disqualification from public employment. In 1975, in *Rock* v. *Secretary of Defense*, a federal district court upheld the revocation of a TOP SECRET industrial security clearance in a case where the deputy manager of an industrial enterprise had publicly acknowledged homosexual activities and had indicated that he would persist in these activities despite the fact that they violated California law. The issue here, said the court, was not whether a homosexual can be denied a security clearance merely because of his homosexuality, but whether an individual may be denied such a clearance on the grounds that he knowingly and openly chose to violate a criminal law—a statute perhaps archaic but until repealed nevertheless part of the law of the land. The court then quoted approvingly from the findings of the hearing examiner and the appeals board:

> Selective obedience to the law, or more aptly, electing to disobey "oppressive laws" and to abide solely by the dictates of one's own conscience does not inspire confidence in applicant's judgment, discretion, reliability or trustworthiness. . . . Although it is too remote to predict that the applicant will violate specific security regulations because he violates law proscribing certain sexual activities, it is both logical and reasonable to infer unreliability and untrustworthiness as well as poor judgment from the deliberate and habitual violation of the law over a long period of time in the face of strong social condemnation. [Such a person may at some time] arrogate unto himself the supposed right to decide not to respect and comply with other laws and regulations.[67]

The finding in the *Rock* case that selective obedience to the law may be incompatible with trustworthiness has obvious implications for membership in Marxist-Leninist organizations that regard the rule of law as a reflection of capitalist oppression and that consider the binding quality of law under capitalism a dispensable aspect of "bourgeois democracy." An applicant for a sensitive position who shares these views may therefore well come to be judged unreliable and untrustworthy. Indeed, there is evidence to indicate that security offi-

67. Rock v. Secretary, Department of Defense, Memorandum Order no. C-74-1128 SC, U.S. District Court, Northern District of California, March 21, 1975, reprinted in Bureau of National Affairs, *Security and Loyalty Reporter*, no. 234 (April 23, 1975), pp. 29: 431-34.

cers at times use just such criteria when faced with applicants whom they have difficulty disqualifying on the grounds of "guilty knowledge and intent."

The crucial importance of reliability and trustworthiness has been affirmed by the courts many times. The judges have stressed that the government, in denying a security clearance, is not under the obligation to demonstrate that classified material *will* be misused by an applicant. "We know of no constitutional requirement," a court of appeals ruled in *Adams* v. *Laird* in 1969, "that the president must, in seeking to safeguard the integrity of classified information, provide that a security clearance must be granted unless it be affirmatively proven that the applicant 'would use' it improperly. We are not in an area of knowledge or experience where absolutes obtain, and the grant or denial of security clearances is an inexact science at best."[68] The standard to be applied is the affirmative finding that clearance is clearly consistent with the national interest. This standard is particular enough to satisfy the requirements of due process. There is no need in such cases for objective and direct *evidence to prove* a nexus between the conduct involved and the denial of a security clearance. It is enough if "there is a rational connection between the facts relied upon and the conclusions drawn."[69]

A review of federal court decisions, as undertaken here, suggests that the courts bear responsibility for some of the difficulties experienced by the loyalty-security program during the last twenty years. The insistence of the courts, for example, that the employability of persons in government service be judged by the same standard that is applied to governmental restrictions on the exercise of First Amendment rights and liberties—the "guilty knowledge and intent" test— has led to consequences that can only be described as farcical. The following exchange during a congressional hearing in 1978 between a Senate Judiciary Committee staff member (Mr. Schultz) and Alan K. Campbell, then chairman of the Civil Service Commission, is a case in point:

> MR. SCHULTZ: I have a . . . question with regard to membership in the Communist Party.
>
> If the Civil Service Commission has information that he is a member of the Communist Party, or the Trotskyites, or the Maoists, but he has not, to the knowledge of the Commission, engaged in any act designed to bring about the violent overthrow of the U.S. Government, nor made statements

68. Adams v. Laird, 420 F. 2d 230, 239 (1969), cert. den. 397 U.S. 1039 (1970).
69. Gayer v. Schlesinger, 490 F. 2d 740, 751 (1973).

concerning such overthrow, is it your position that he could not be denied employment? . . . Is that correct?

MR. CAMPBELL: Yes, I believe that is correct.

MR. SCHULTZ: Suppose an applicant was a member of the Puerto Rican Socialist Party, which is really a Castro Communist Party that openly acclaims and supports the terrorist activities carried out by the Puerto Rican terrorist organization, the FALN. A recent raid on a Chicago bomb factory established that members of the Puerto Rican Socialist Party have actually been involved in terrorist activities of the FALN. The Puerto Rican Socialist Party, in addition, supports the Castro government and maintains a permanent office in Havana. . . . Does such membership disqualify an applicant from employment in a non-sensitive or sensitive government position?

MR. CAMPBELL: Standing alone as mere membership the information would not disqualify him.[70]

In actual fact, it is of course unlikely that many members of such organizations, especially those with foreign ties, would slip through the screening net. Some other grounds, involving lack of suitability, would perhaps be used to keep them out. Nevertheless, a legal situation that forces the government to forgo using the security and loyalty criteria of existing regulations breeds, if not laxness, at least subterfuge and hypocrisy. Neither is desirable or necessary.

Some of the more restrictive court rulings have come in the context of nonsensitive positions, such as resident physicians in VA hospitals where considerations of security have little place anyway. No court case so far has tested the exclusion of, say, a member of the Communist party from a truly sensitive position or the asking of questions about membership in such an organization in a personnel investigation for a critical-sensitive position. As far as access to classified information is concerned, the rulings of the courts appear to leave room for a rigorous screening program. Many of the problems that have developed, as we will see in the following pages, are primarily political or are the unforeseen consequences of legislation not meant to apply specifically to the area of loyalty and security.

70. Senate, Subcommittee on Criminal Laws of the Committee on the Judiciary, *Hearings on Erosion of Law Enforcement Intelligence*, p. 217.

4

The Impaired Data Base

Probably the most serious problem facing the federal loyalty-security program today is the lack of an adequate data base that could help agencies and OPM make determinations concerning the loyalty of applicants and employees. This situation is the result of several developments, including the abolition of the attorney general's list of subversive organizations in 1974.

The Demise of the Attorney General's List

The origins of the attorney general's list go back to the Deportation and Exclusion laws of 1917, 1918, and 1920, which forbade any alien to enter or to remain in the United States if he belonged to a group that advocated the violent overthrow of the government. New interest in focusing the spotlight of exposure on un-American activities developed in the 1930s out of concern over the efforts of Hitler's propaganda machine to capture public opinion in this country. The enactment of the Foreign Agents Registration Act of 1938,[1] of Section 9-A of the Hatch Act of 1939,[2] and of the Voorhis Anti-Propaganda Act in 1940[3] all reflected apprehension of the political activities of individuals and groups who sought to advance their interests through resort to violence and by subterfuge that hid their foreign connections. In addition to American fascist groups, "un-American activities" always included the American Communist party and its various front organizations.[4]

From the beginning, the endeavor to compile lists of "un-American" or subversive organizations had two purposes—to help keep active members of such groups out of government employment and to inform the public at large of the clandestine goals of these movements.

1. 52 Stat. 631, 22 U.S.C. 611.
2. 53 Stat. 1148, 5 U.S.C. 118j.
3. 54 Stat. 1201, 18 U.S.C. 2386.
4. For a fuller discussion see Eleanor Bontecou, *The Federal Loyalty-Security Program* (Ithaca, N.Y.: Cornell University Press, 1953), pp. 159-67.

Both of these aims enjoyed wide support from conservatives as well as liberals. A study undertaken in 1945 by the Brookings Institution called attention to the need to expose un-American activities that were defined as secretly promoting the interests of a foreign nation or association.[5] After the publication in 1948 of the list of subversive organizations mandated by Executive Order (EO) 9835, President Truman's loyalty program, the noted civil liberties lawyer Morris L. Ernst supported the public availability of such a list, compiled after hearings, which would include organizations that had failed to make full disclosure of finances, membership, officers, and activities. The marketplace of ideas, Ernst argued, is corrupted by the pumping in of ideas with no one knowing who the backers of these ideas are.[6]

EO 9835 of March 21, 1947, directed the Department of Justice to develop a list of foreign and domestic organizations

> which the Attorney General, after appropriate investigation and determination, designates as totalitarian, fascist, communist or subversive, or as having adopted a policy of advocating or approving the commission of acts of force or violence to deny others their rights under the Constitution of the United States or as seeking to alter the form of government of the United States by unconstitutional means.[7]

The list, published in the *Federal Register* of March 20, 1948,[8] contained the names of 82 organizations, 47 of which had been compiled by Attorney General Francis Biddle during the war years. The practice of designating organizations according to six categories, corresponding to the six classes of organizations described in EO 9835, was abandoned after the promulgation of EO 10450 in 1953. By 1955 the list had grown to over 200 organizations, listed alphabetically. No new group was added to the list after 1955. By then the great majority of the organizations listed were Communist.

The announced purpose of the list, according to its preamble, was to provide information for "Federal civilian officers and employees" and to serve "the convenience of persons completing applications for Federal employment. Membership in or affiliation with a designated organization is one factor to be considered by the departments and agencies of the Federal Government in connection with the employ-

5. Brookings Institution, *Suggested Standards for Determining Un-American Activities* (Washington, D.C.: Brookings Institution, 1945), pp. 6-7.

6. Morris L. Ernst, "Some Affirmative Suggestions for a Loyalty Program," in John C. Wahlke, ed., *Loyalty in a Democratic Society* (Boston: D. C. Heath, 1952), pp. 61, 64.

7. Part III, paragraph 3, of EO 9835, March 21, 1947, 12 F.R. 1935.

8. "Attorney General's List," 13 F.R. 1473.

ment or retention in employment of individuals in federal service." In other words, a person's association with a group on the list was not an automatic bar to employment but a warning signal requiring investigation to determine the circumstances of the affiliation and its bearing upon the person's loyalty. The observance of this injunction against guilt by association has varied over time and, as one would expect, has fluctuated with the country's concern about Communist penetration. In the 1950s association with an organization on the list carried more weight than in the early 1970s.

The attorney general's list survived several challenges to its constitutionality. In the best-known case, *Joint Anti-Fascist Refugee Committee* v. *McGrath*, decided in 1951,[9] the Supreme Court found that the lack of notice and hearing for the listed organizations violated the due process clause of the Fifth Amendment, but only Justice Black subscribed to the view that the list itself violated the First Amendment by punishing members of the listed organizations for their political beliefs and that it constituted an unconstitutional bill of attainder. As a result of the *McGrath* decision, Attorney General Herbert Brownell in 1953 issued rules providing for both notice and hearing.[10] The great majority of the listed organizations, however, did not request an opportunity to contest. Many of them may no longer have been in existence when the opportunity to challenge the listing was provided, for these organizations have often had only a short life. The National Lawyers Guild, often referred to as the legal arm of the Communist party, upon receiving notice of proposed designation, filed an ultimately unsuccessful court suit.[11]

By 1970, according to Assistant Attorney General Robert C. Mardian, head of the Justice Department's Internal Security Division,[12] most of the listed organizations were defunct. Only ten organizations were still active, while three others were in existence but showed little activity. It was in part to remedy this situation that President Nixon issued EO 11605 on July 2, 1971.[13] The order expanded and more clearly defined the criteria for listing an organization and made the Subversive Activities Control Board, created by Title I of the Internal

9. Joint Anti-Fascist Refugee Committee v. McGrath, 341 U.S. 123 (1951).

10. Attorney General's Order No. 11-53, May 6, 1953, 18 F.R. 2619.

11. National Lawyers Guild v. Brownell, 225 F. 2d 552 (1955), cert. denied 351 U.S. 927 (1956).

12. Letter to Congressman Richard H. Ichord of November 30, 1971, reproduced in U.S. Congress, House, Committee on Internal Security, *Hearings Regarding the Administration of the Subversive Activities Control Act of 1950 and the Federal Civilian Employee Loyalty-Security Program*, part 1, 91st Cong., 2d sess., 1971, pp. 5263-64. A copy of the attorney general's list can be found on pp. 5256-63.

13. 36 F.R. 12831.

Security Act of 1950,[14] the fact-finding agency with authority to add and remove groups after an evidentiary hearing. Upon petition of the attorney general, the board could also declare listed organizations defunct.

An action for a declaration that EO 11605 and the attorney general's list were unconstitutional, filed by nine organizations including the Communist party, was dismissed by a federal district court as unripe in *American Servicemen's Union* v. *Mitchell* in 1972. The executive order, the court acknowledged, contained "definitions governing listing that appear on their face to raise constitutional problems by reason of their vagueness and overbreadth and the resulting effect on the right of many Government workers, present or future." But these "difficult and extremely troublesome matters" were not yet ripe for determination. Some of the suing organizations were not presently on the list; no showing had been made that the members of any of the nine organizations were seeking employment or were employed by the federal government. The claimed chilling effect on First Amendment freedoms was "premised more on political intuition than on legal developments of which the Court can take legal cognizance."[15]

The delegation of responsibility for the list to the Subversive Activities Control Board came at a time when that agency had become largely idle. Protracted hearings on the registration of the Communist party and various front organizations, mandated by the Internal Security Act of 1950, had led to equally protracted court suits—all of them inconclusive in their outcome. Congress, convinced that the board was wasting the taxpayers' money without being able to show concrete accomplishments, in 1972 therefore passed legislation that forbade the use of federal money for the implementation of EO 11605.[16] In his budget message for fiscal year 1974, President Nixon did not request any funds for the Subversive Activities Control Board, and it therefore ceased to function on June 30, 1973.

A year later, the attorney general's list itself was quietly laid to rest by President Nixon's EO 11785, issued on June 4, 1974, which provided in Section 2:

> Neither the Attorney General, nor the Subversive Activities Control Board, nor any other agency shall designate organizations pursuant to section 12 of Executive Order 10450, as amended, nor circulate nor publish a list of organizations previously so designated. The list of organizations previously

14. Subversive Activities Control Act, 64 Stat. 987, 50 U.S.C. 781.

15. American Servicemen's Union v. Mitchell, 54 F.R.D. 14, 17-18 (1972).

16. 86 Stat. 1109 (1972).

designated is hereby abolished and shall not be used for any purpose.[17]

The prime mover for the abolition of the list is said to have been Attorney General William B. Saxbe, who had concluded that the list, hopelessly out of date, no longer served any useful purpose.

It may well be that the list, as it had evolved by 1974, no longer served a useful objective. There appears to be widespread support, however, for the view that the absence of any kind of central guidance has made the operation of the loyalty-security program very difficult. "In terms of organizational affiliations," CSC Chairman Kimbell Johnson told Congress in 1970, "the government is practically without a yardstick at this time. The Attorney General's list has not been amended in 15 years." Asked to comment on the utility of the list, he went on to say that the list provided "a yardstick which has limited but decided utility, in terms of determining what cases shall be investigated by the FBI and second in the adjudication of the case. Certainly once it is so designated the general public knows that it has been authoritatively cited that it is subversive in nature."[18] The abolition of the list eliminated these functions and left both government agencies and individuals without any meaningful assistance in making sense of the large and ever-changing number of Communist front groups that hide their true purposes from the public. The mask of anonymity worn by members of these organizations, as Justice Frankfurter pointed out in 1961, "serves the double purpose of protecting them from popular prejudice and of enabling them to cover over a foreign directed conspiracy, infiltrate into other groups, and enlist the support of persons who would not, if the truth were revealed, lend their support."[19] It is somewhat unfair, argued a liberal critic of the Truman loyalty program back in 1953, when the government, "having knowledge of the communist connections and disloyal purposes of a group which is seeking to deceive the public, keeps that knowledge to itself, yet penalizes those who have innocently taken the organization at its face value."[20]

To be sure, membership in a suspect organization neither has been in the past nor is today considered conclusive proof of disloyalty. Yet for an individual to demonstrate that he was deceived and did not know the true purpose of such a group may at times be difficult. As

17. EO 11785, June 4, 1974, 39 F.R. 20053.

18. See House, Committee on Internal Security, *Hearings Regarding the Subversive Activities Control Act*, p. 5254.

19. Communist Party v. Subversive Activities Control Board, 367 U.S. 1, 102-103 (1961).

20. Bontecou, *Loyalty-Security Program*, p. 203.

Professor Ralph S. Brown, another liberal critic of the loyalty-security program, pointed out in 1958, it is also "a wasteful and burdensome process. Considerable expertness about these matters is supposed to exist on the government's side. To have it compiled and available would permit quick evaluation of most affiliations."[21] Today the government probably no longer has as much information on Communist-controlled organizations as Professor Brown in 1958 expected it to possess, but this defect could be remedied by the development of carefully researched and detailed information—not mere lists—on organizations that have been penetrated and are controlled by the Communist party or similar groups.

The abolition of the attorney general's list also has deprived OPM of any help in deciding when it should refer loyalty cases to the FBI for further investigation, as required by Section 8(d) of EO 10450, and it has left the FBI without guidance on what the bureau should be looking for in conducting these investigations. For understandable reasons, the FBI today interprets its domestic security function—a subject examined later in this study—in the narrowest possible terms. This attitude of great caution is even more pronounced when it comes to loyalty investigations, where the FBI for all practical purposes no longer plays a real role. This creates problems. The government cannot screen people for sensitive positions without accurate information about the significance of affiliations with various political organizations, and this judgment presupposes accurate and up-to-date knowledge about the aims and purposes of these groups. Objectionable as it may be to many people, somebody in the government therefore will have to shoulder the task of compiling this kind of intelligence.

The Consequences of the Privacy Act and of the Freedom of Information Act

The enactment of the Privacy Act of 1974 was in large measure the result of efforts made by Senator Sam Ervin and his Subcommittee on Constitutional Rights to ensure that the government does not maintain secret records about individuals. Hearings held by the Ervin committee in 1971 and 1972 had given widespread publicity to the existence of military record centers that contained extensive files on the political activities of civilians not connected with the military services. Army intelligence alone was said to have had records on more than 100,000 civilians unaffiliated with the armed forces. Much of this extensive volume of data, the committee charged, contained fragmen-

---

21. Ralph S. Brown, Jr., *Loyalty and Security: Employment Tests in the United States* (New Haven, Conn.: Yale University Press, 1958), p. 297.

tary, incorrect, and irrelevant information, such as material on the subjects' financial affairs and sex lives, that could not be considered intelligence in any meaningful sense of the word and went far beyond the ostensible purpose of this system of surveillance and data collection—the putting down of civil disturbances in the cities.[22] The Privacy Act, signed into law on December 31, 1974, was intended to prevent such abuses. It requires that

- each agency of the government annually provide public notice in the *Federal Register* of the kinds of records it maintains
- only such records be compiled as are necessary to accomplish the agency's purpose, and records be maintained with timeliness and accuracy to ensure fairness
- individuals be given the right of access to records about themselves as well as the right to dispute and correct records they regard as inaccurate
- personal information not be disclosed without the written consent of the individual concerned
- no agency, unless expressly authorized, maintain records describing how an individual exercises rights guaranteed by the First Amendment

Both civil and criminal sanctions are provided for violations of these provisions.[23]

The Privacy Act has affected the loyalty-security program in several ways. First, it has diminished the availability of state and local law enforcement data needed in background investigations of applicants for government positions. In many instances, the damaging effect of the Privacy Act has been made worse by other statutes hampering the collection of information, such as the Fair Credit Reporting Act of 1970[24] and the Family Educational Rights and Privacy Act of 1974,[25] which have made it difficult to obtain previously available information from banks, credit bureaus, collection agencies, and educational institutions. Furthermore, many states have by now enacted their own privacy laws, some of them patterned on the federal statute or going beyond it. About 80 percent of the states today have established some restrictions on the dissemination of criminal justice information. On occasion, the problem has not been what the various laws themselves

22. See U.S. Congress, Senate, Subcommittee on Constitutional Rights of the Committee on the Judiciary, *Hearings on Data Banks, Computers and the Bill of Rights,* 92d Cong., 1st sess., February-March 1971; *Military Surveillance of Civilian Politics,* Report, 93d Cong., 1st sess., 1973.

23. Public Law 93-579, 88 Stat. 1896, 5 U.S.C. 552a.

24. 84 Stat. 1128, 15 U.S.C. 1681.

25. 88 Stat. 484, 20 U.S.C. 1232g.

permit but what the custodians of records perceive them to mean. A case in point is the misinterpretation by many state officials of a regulation concerning the dissemination of nonconviction data issued by the Law Enforcement Assistance Administration (LEAA) in 1976.

"The mere fact that a man has been arrested," the Supreme Court ruled in 1957, "has very little, if any, probative value in showing that he has engaged in any misconduct."[26] Citing this holding with approval, a federal district court pronounced in 1971: "Under our system of criminal justice, only a conviction carries legal significance as to a person's involvement in criminal behavior."[27] In line with this reasoning, many states and localities today forbid the release of arrest records and permit the disclosure of conviction data only. Reflecting the same concern about damaging the privacy rights of individuals and implementing a congressional mandate, the LEAA in 1976 issued a regulation that required agencies receiving LEAA funds to ensure that the dissemination of nonconviction data is limited to (1) criminal justice agencies and (2) "individuals and agencies for any purpose authorized by the statute, ordinance, Executive Order, or court rule, decision or order, as construed by appropriate State or local officials or agencies."[28] In the absence of a federal statute or executive order specifically authorizing the collection of criminal history information, many states and local agencies today limit the release of such information to conviction data. A study undertaken for DOD in 1978 showed that only seventeen states allowed the release of both conviction and nonconviction data to DOD personnel investigators and fifteen states released only conviction data.[29] OPM investigators face similar difficulties.

The restriction of the release of criminal history information to conviction records has a deleterious effect on security investigations. A record of arrest without conviction does not, of course, establish proof of misconduct, but it may indicate a significant investigative issue that requires resolution. Many arrests for offenses that persons actually commit do not result in convictions because a key witness refuses to testify or because the victim of the offense decides not to press charges, or for many other reasons not at all related to the guilt or innocence of the accused. A recent LEAA study showed that more than one-half of all felony arrests referred to prosecutors in thirteen

26. Schware v. Board of Examiners, 353 U.S. 232, 241 (1957).

27. Menard v. Mitchell, 328 F. Supp. 718, 724 (1971).

28. 28 C.F.R. 20.21.

29. SEARCH Group, Inc., *Federal Access to State and Local Criminal Justice Information for Federal Personnel Security and Employment Suitability Determinations* (Sacramento, Calif.: SEARCH Group, 1979), p. 24.

jurisdictions were either rejected for prosecution or dismissed a short time later.[30] It is, therefore, probable that the denial of arrest data deprives adjudicators of personnel security of highly significant information relevant to the determination of a person's reliability and trustworthiness.

There are other problems. Even where the release of arrest records is authorized, investigators often encounter prolonged delays in obtaining these data. In the state of Massachusetts, for example, the commissioner of probation, under whose jurisdiction the records are, told the Defense Investigative Service (DIS) in 1978 that he could accept no more than six checks at a time and that he did not know when he could get the results since DIS access was equal to that of school bus drivers, the alcoholic beverage commission, and other applicants, all part of a group having the lowest priority. DIS at that time was conducting about 500 security investigations a week in Massachusetts and for all practical purposes was therefore completely frustrated in getting the promised access.[31] Recently concluded negotiations are expected to improve this unfortunate situation. Service recruiters who are supposed to verify the information provided by prospective enlistees on enlistment forms often encounter the same difficulties. Additional complications arise here because most enlistees are seventeen to twenty-one years of age, and juvenile justice data are especially hard to obtain. Some states bar their release entirely; in other jurisdictions nonconviction records can be purged or sealed.[32]

Both OPM and DIS make applicants complete release forms that are designed to help investigators obtain the needed information. Both agencies also take the position that personnel investigations are an authorized law enforcement activity since they enforce the rules and regulations of the civil service and because they are the means of ensuring the exclusion of security risks and persons convicted of certain criminal offenses who are barred by statute from federal employment. Still, serious problems of access remain, especially for OPM. The problems arising from this situation are grave because the responsibility of OPM includes the screening of individuals to positions of critical sensitivity in the federal government. These persons will work in nuclear research, rocketry, criminal law enforcement, policy devel-

30. Testimony of Thomas J. O'Brien, director for security plans and programs, DOD, before the Subcommittee on Oversight of the House Permanent Select Committee on Intelligence, *Hearings on Pre-Employment Security Procedures of the Intelligence Agencies,* 96th Cong., 1st sess., June 21, 1979, p. 190.

31. Testimony of Bernard J. O'Donnell, director, DIS, ibid., p. 193.

32. U.S. Department of Justice, LEAA, *Privacy and Security of Criminal History Information: Compendium of State Legislation* (Washington, D.C., 1978), pp. 32-33.

opment, and fiduciary or other duties requiring the highest level of public trust. The accuracy and completeness of the information developed in personnel investigations also has an important effect on the fairness of adjudications. Even though a thorough investigation does not guarantee a sound decision, an incomplete investigation clearly makes a fair decision impossible.

The second major way in which the Privacy Act has affected the loyalty-security program involves the growing reluctance of persons to provide information to personnel investigators. In accordance with the Privacy Act, witnesses interviewed must be advised of the use that will be made of the information provided by them, including the possibility that the information may be made available upon request to the person who is being investigated.[33] Understandably, interviewees hesitate to provide unfavorable information because they fear disclosure as well as the possibility of liability in a civil suit. Section (k)(5) of the Privacy Act provides for granting confidentiality to a source, but OMB guidelines caution that the legislative history of the act would allow withholding the identity of sources from the subject only under very limited circumstances. Furthermore, intelligent persons who have followed the implementation of the Freedom of Information Act and the Privacy Act know that promises of confidentiality can be overturned by judicial decision or nullified by mere human error. As the Department of Justice told the Senate Judiciary Committee in 1978: "In theory, the acts provide an adequate basis for protecting our sources, but whether they in fact do so is largely irrelevant as long as *our sources think* they do not."[34]

The reluctance to cooperate with personnel investigators was documented in a report prepared by the General Accounting Office, issued November 1978. The examples concern FBI investigations, but there is no reason to think that OPM or DIS background investigators do not experience similar difficulties.

• During a background investigation of a nominee for U.S. district judge, the FBI questioned two attorneys, but both were extremely reluctant to furnish their opinions of the nominee's qualifications. They feared that if the nominee was appointed and later learned of their comments, he would use his position to punish them. The attorneys had little confidence in the confidentiality protection afforded by the Freedom of Information and the Privacy acts, but eventually pro-

33. 5 U.S.C. 552a(e)(3)(B).

34. U.S. Congress, Senate, Subcommittee on Criminal Laws and Procedures of the Committee on the Judiciary, *Hearings on the Erosion of Law Enforcement Intelligence and Its Impact on the Public Security,* part 8, 95th Cong., 2d sess., 1978, p. 32.

vided some comments. The FBI indicated, however, that there was no assurance that they were as candid as they might have been before passage of these acts.

- In more than forty interviews conducted during an FBI background investigation for a possible presidential appointment, the agents believed that in over half of the interviews possibly derogatory information was being withheld. On many occasions the agents were asked if the appointee would have access to the information through the Privacy Act. Several of the individuals interviewed said that they feared reprisals and would not make derogatory comments.

- An FBI office reported that the most significant negative effect on its investigative mission resulted from a $600,000 lawsuit filed against a person who, about twenty years ago, allegedly provided derogatory information to the FBI about the plaintiff's suitability for a government job. The plaintiff had used the Freedom of Information Act to request FBI files that, she asserted, allowed her to identify the source of the derogatory information. The plaintiff charged that the information was slanderous and defamatory. The suit was dismissed because the statute of limitations had run out, but the primary issue of whether or not a person can sue someone who has provided information to the FBI was never addressed or resolved. Numerous individuals informed FBI agents that, as a result of this lawsuit, they would never provide derogatory information to the FBI.

- In an investigation of an FBI applicant, a local police official refused to provide derogatory information concerning the applicant. The official said that under the Freedom of Information Act the applicant would have access to the information and, even if his identity were to remain confidential, the information could serve to identify him.

- FBI agents questioned the former employer of a person applying for an FBI position. Company officials provided the dates of employment, but refused to provide a recommendation or comment on the employee's performance, citing the Privacy Act and the fact that the information could become known to the applicant. The officials further stated that no other information would be provided regarding the applicant even if the applicant signed a release form.

- The FBI learned that an FBI applicant was a former employee of a midwestern state's bureau of investigation. State bureau officials acknowledged they had derogatory information concerning the applicant but refused to reveal the information because the applicant would have access to it under the Privacy Act.[35]

35. U.S. General Accounting Office (GAO), *Impact of the Freedom of Information and Privacy Acts on Law Enforcement Agencies*, GGD-78-108, November 15, 1978, pp. 15-17, 23.

In its report, the General Accounting Office raised the question whether these instances of reluctance to provide information resulted solely from the Freedom of Information and the Privacy acts or whether other regulations and administrative policies as well as a general distrust of law enforcement agencies might have had as much or more to do with the FBI's difficulties. Whether or not these acts are indeed the sole culprits, it seems undeniable that both statutes, enacted for good and worthy reasons, have had unforeseen consequences and have created distinct and identifiable difficulties for law enforcement agents in general and personnel background investigators in particular.

The right of the subject of such an investigation to have access to his investigative file not only contributes to the reluctance of persons to provide unfavorable information, but may also facilitate the ability of agents of foreign powers or other subversives to infiltrate the government. Such access enhances the citizen's ability to protect himself against dishonest informers and possibly erroneous and damaging information. As Professor Ralph S. Brown pointed out in 1958, however, problems arise in determining the good faith of persons who apply for access to their files: "The security officers would argue with some reason that an unrestricted process would permit every Communist to inquire what the FBI had on him."[36] Finding no derogatory information in his file, such a person would then feel emboldened to attempt to gain appointment or promotion to the most sensitive position. Going beyond the most daring dreams of liberal critics of the loyalty-security program in the 1950s, today the Freedom of Information and the Privacy acts provide just such access to investigative files. The benefits to the public of open files are obvious; the costs paid for them in terms of a personnel security program of diminished effectiveness are more difficult to measure.

The third, and perhaps most serious, deleterious effect of the Privacy Act on the loyalty-security program involves the difficulties created by the act for the maintenance of records. In the past, under the Housekeeping Act of 1789,[37] an agency was permitted to keep whatever records and files it deemed necessary to accomplish the agency's mission. The Privacy Act imposed far more limiting rules. In addition to the requirements of accuracy, timeliness, and access, Section (e)(7) of the act provides that agencies "maintain no record describing how any individual exercises rights guaranteed by the First Amendment unless expressly authorized by statute or by the individ-

36. Brown, *Loyalty and Security*, p. 304, n. 19.
37. 5 U.S.C. 22.

ual about whom the record is maintained or unless pertinent to and within the scope of an authorized law enforcement activity." This section of the act has led to the closing down of entire categories of record systems.

The Security Research and Analysis Section (SRAS) of OPM, until its abolition in 1980, was in charge of compiling an extensive data base on subversive organizations and their members and associates. The most important part of this operation was the security index, an investigative leads file containing information on Communist and other subversive activities. The origin of this index went back to the screening for war service appointments in 1940–1941; by the early 1970s it had grown to more than 2 million entries providing leads to documents relating to both organizations and individuals. These materials had been developed from the published hearings of congressional committees, state legislative committees, various public investigative bodies, and the publications of subversive organizations. In congressional testimony given in 1970, CSC Chairman Kimbell Johnson praised the index as an important investigative tool. "The effectiveness of this file is evidenced by the fact that approximately 20 percent of the cases we refer to the FBI for a full field investigation by that Bureau are referred because of information developed from a research of this file."[38] Anthony L. Mondello, general counsel of CSC, called it a "valuable adjunct" to the security investigations index, the master file of all personnel investigations conducted since 1939.[39]

After the enactment of the Privacy Act, Robert J. Drummond, director of the Bureau of Personnel Investigations, in a memorandum dated February 18, 1975, proposed that the CSC discontinue the maintenance and use of the security index. The act, he pointed out, required that the CSC list the index in the *Federal Register* and make it possible for individuals to gain access to and contest any records pertaining to them. "Aside from the administrative burden in complying with the above provisions, publishing the categories of individuals on whom records are maintained would have the effect of informing the public that we are keeping records on private citizens." The index was not authorized by any specific statutory or executive order, and it clearly pertained to the way individuals exercised their First Amendment rights. Even if the CSC were to take the position, Drummond argued, that keeping this file was an essential part of the commission's investigatory responsibilities, "I think to keep the file would expose us

38. See House, Committee on Internal Security, *Hearings Regarding the Subversive Activities Control Act*, p. 5233.
39. Ibid., p. 5889.

to innumerable court challenges."[40] CSC Chairman Robert E. Hampton at first was not sure that the index should be abolished. "Will the government lose a valuable tool designed to protect our national security?" he asked in a memorandum to Drummond dated March 6, 1975.[41] After further deliberation, however, Hampton agreed with Drummond's position, and on September 8, 1975, it was decided to remove the cards on individuals from the index. After objections from several members of Congress, the decision to destroy these cards and materials was changed to placing them in warehouse storage.

For a time, the SRAS was allowed to continue to maintain files on organizations. When an investigation disclosed that a subject was a member of an organization not known to the investigator or evaluator, the name of the organization was checked against the index of organizations. The subject's membership, however, was included in the investigative report only if that person was found to have engaged in illegal activity, that is, (1) denied a person's rights guaranteed by the Constitution, (2) engaged in or advocated the violent overthrow of the government, or (3) committed crimes against property or persons. To note membership alone, without any other adverse information, Mr. Drummond told a congressional committee in 1978, "would amount to maintaining records on how people exercise their first amendment rights, and this is precluded by the Privacy Act." When asked whether this was true for any level of appointment the applicant was being considered for, Mr. Drummond replied: "That is true."[42]

As late as December 1973, the chief of SRAS, W. ("Rush") Yarosh, had been praised by his superior for his extensive experience, knowledge, and expertise in the security field and recommended for promotion. A few years later, in the changed political climate of the post-Watergate period and Congress's attacks on the intelligence agencies, the very existence of a CSC security section and of files on subversives had become a political liability and a source of embarrassment. By then the personnel of the section, at one time approximately thirty-five persons, had been reduced to the section chief and two low-level assistants. Finally, in September 1980, the SRAS was abolished, and its remaining records were put in storage. Since then, OPM no longer has files against which personnel investigators or evaluators could check suspect political affiliations. The consequences of the discontinuance of this important investigative tool are all the more serious in view of

40. Robert J. Drummond, Jr., to CSC, February 18, 1975.
41. Robert E. Hampton to Robert J. Drummond, March 6, 1975.
42. Senate, Subcommittee on Criminal Laws of the Committee on the Judiciary, *Hearings on Erosion of Law Enforcement Intelligence*, part 4, p. 217.

the almost total abandonment of loyalty investigations by the FBI and of the bureau's sharp curtailment of its own data base in this area.

The Reduced Domestic Intelligence Function of the FBI

The investigation of extremist and subversive groups and individuals by the FBI goes back to the 1930s. The terms "domestic intelligence" and "internal security" have been used interchangeably to describe this activity, conducted for both intelligence and prosecution purposes. The term "extremists" has included the Ku Klux Klan, various Nazi organizations, and, later, militant black groups; "subversives" has meant primarily the radical Left.

The legal basis for FBI domestic security investigations includes, first, the criminal statutes in Title 18 of the United States Code, which penalize crimes such as assaulting or murdering a federal official, conspiring to overthrow the government, damaging government property, transporting explosives in interstate commerce, and much more. The collection of intelligence here is part of the government's responsibility to detect and punish as well as to prevent crimes. The responsibility of the executive branch to prevent crimes, the courts have held, is inherent in the president's constitutional authority to take care that the laws be faithfully executed (Article II, Section 3) and in the obligation of the federal government to protect the states against domestic violence (Article IV, Section 4).[43]

A second basis for the investigation of subversives and extremists is a series of presidential directives and statements made by President Roosevelt to FBI director J. Edgar Hoover in 1936, 1938, and 1939. There is some question whether Roosevelt was concerned mainly with groups under foreign influence, but the phrase "subversive activities" is used several times without qualifications and entailed a sweeping mandate. The investigation of subversives included physical surveillance, elaborate record keeping, mail covers, and mail openings; a whole generation of FBI agents came to regard these techniques as routine in both foreign and domestic intelligence collection.[44]

From the beginning, "subversive activities" included more than violent conduct or the violation of specific criminal statutes and took in the various activities of fascist and Communist groups as such. In

43. Office of the Attorney General, memorandum, "Authority of the FBI to Undertake Domestic Security Investigations," March 31, 1977, reprinted in U.S. Congress, House, Subcommittee on Civil and Constitutional Rights of the Committee on the Judiciary, *Hearings on FBI Oversight*, 95th Cong., 1st sess., 1977, pp. 222-26.

44. Richard E. Morgan, *Domestic Intelligence: Monitoring Dissent in America* (Austin: University of Texas Press, 1980), pp. 30-36.

response to a GAO report in 1976, which suggested that FBI domestic intelligence investigations be confined to anticipating violence, the FBI defended its broad jurisdiction in this area in the following way:

> Limiting domestic intelligence investigation to preventing force and violence could restrict the gathering of intelligence information useful for anticipating threats to national security of a more subtle nature. This is the case because, in our view, such a limitation would protect from governmental inquiry those plotting to undermine our institutions during their preliminary stages of organization and preparation and thus inhibit the development of an intelligence collage upon which to base meaningful analysis and predictions as to future threats to the stability of our society.[45]

A third source of FBI authority for domestic intelligence gathering was the loyalty-security program. One of the reasons why President Roosevelt wanted the FBI to investigate subversive groups, such as the Communist party, is said to have been his concern that members of such groups might seek to gain responsible positions in government.[46] In 1941, the FBI was allocated money specifically for the investigation of federal employees who were members of subversive organizations.[47] This responsibility was reaffirmed in the Truman and Eisenhower loyalty-security programs. EO 10450 quite explicitly required the FBI to check the names of all applicants and incumbents of the executive branch against its records (the National Agency Check), and to conduct full field investigations where such checks had revealed questionable loyalty or other threats to the national security. In order to meet this responsibility, the FBI collected the identity of all persons connected with subversive or extremist activities and their degree of involvement—the length of membership, positions held, attendance at meetings, fund-raising or recruiting activities, and so on. Information about subversive groups also was provided to the attorney general to help him compile his list of subversive organizations, mandated by EO 9835 of 1947, and as evidence for hearings before the Subversive Activities Control Board.[48]

45. FBI comments on draft of GAO, *FBI Domestic Intelligence Operations—Their Purpose and Scope: Issues That Need to Be Resolved*, GGD-76-50, February 24, 1976, p. 213.

46. John T. Elliff, *The Reform of FBI Intelligence Activities* (Princeton, N.J.: Princeton University Press, 1979), p. 152.

47. Bontecou, *Loyalty-Security Program*, p. 10.

48. Memorandum from Glen E. Pommerening, assistant attorney general for administration, to FBI Director Clarence M. Kelley, November 17, 1974, quoted in U.S. Congress, Senate, Select Committee to Study Governmental Operations with Regard to Intelligence Activities [Church committee], *Final Report*, 94th Cong., 2d sess., book III, p. 435.

No new organizations were added to the attorney general's list after 1955, but the FBI's investigation of subversive groups and individuals continued as a means of monitoring the political background of prospective federal employees. In fact, these investigations had never been limited to groups on that list. As a substitute for designation on the attorney general's list, the FBI now provided to other government agencies a "characterization" or "thumb-nail sketch" of groups membership in which was considered ground for possible disqualification from public employment under EO 10450. When President Nixon abolished the attorney general's list in EO 11785 of 1974, the Justice Department instructed the FBI to continue to monitor organizations "engaged in illegal activities or potentially illegal activities."[49]

At the same time, the Justice Department ordered a certain narrowing of the FBI's domestic intelligence jurisdiction. In order to comply with court decisions limiting dismissal from public employment to members of organizations with "guilty knowledge and intent" to commit illegal acts, EO 11785 had eliminated from the potentially disqualifying criteria of EO 10450 membership in Communist or subversive organizations and had substituted for it "knowing membership with the specific intent of furthering the aims" of organizations unlawfully involved in the commission of acts of force or violence. In line with this change, and continuing a policy in force since 1973, the Justice Department told the FBI that while it was "not possible to set definite parameters covering the initiation of investigations of potential organizations falling within the Order, . . . once the investigation reaches a stage that offers a basis for determining that the activities are legal in nature, then the investigation should cease."[50] From now on illegal activity was to be the main basis for domestic security investigations.

The pace of change quickened after the revelation in the early 1970s of various improper FBI activities including special surveillance, electronic eavesdropping, and the use of "dirty tricks" such as leaking false information about targeted individuals, directing informants to disrupt the activities of certain organizations, setting one group of militants against another, and much else. Developed originally as part of the FBI's counterintelligence program (COINTELPRO) against the Communist party, these techniques eventually had been extended to other targets as well.[51] Prodded by congressional and media critics,

49. Ibid., p. 555.
50. Ibid.
51. For full details see the reports of the Church committee. For an attempt to set these abuses in context, see David Martin, "Investigating the FBI," Policy Review, no. 18 (Fall 1981), pp. 113-32.

Attorney General Edward H. Levi now moved not only to put an end to such practices and to reform FBI investigative techniques but also to curtail the scope of domestic security investigations, which, many argued, had run out of control. The federal loyalty-security program, Levi instructed the FBI, was no longer to serve as a basis for such investigations. EO 10450 authorized the investigation of executive branch employees and applicants but not the collection of information so as to have a data base for checking out applicants for federal jobs.[52]

The illegal activity yardstick was one of the key elements in Attorney General Levi's new guidelines for domestic security investigations issued in the spring of 1976. Such investigations were to be conducted only "to ascertain information on the activities of individuals, or the activities of groups, which involve the use of violence and involve or will involve the violation of federal law." This criminal predicate covered activities such as overthrowing the government and depriving persons of their civil rights under the Constitution.[53]

The Levi guidelines ended forty years of far-flung and often rather free-wheeling FBI investigations of subversive political activities. As a result of the new guidelines, the number of groups and individuals investigated and the extent of FBI agents and informant resources devoted to domestic intelligence declined sharply. This decline had begun around 1973 as a result of reduced militancy on the part of various dissident groups and tighter criteria for initiating investigations, but the decrease became decisively more marked after the introduction of the Levi guidelines. On June 30, 1975, a total of 9,814 domestic intelligence investigative matters had been pending; by June 30, 1977, that number had been reduced to 642. During 1974, the FBI had had under investigation 157 subversive and extremist organizations; by early October 1977 that number was down to 17. In November 1974, the FBI had contact with 1,100 domestic intelligence informants; by October 18, 1977, there were about 100 such informants.[54] Domestic security squads in various field offices were disbanded. FBI Director Clarence M. Kelley reported in January 1978 that as a result of the reduced domestic intelligence caseload during fiscal year 1977 the following savings had been achieved: 279 agent work-years, 195 support work-years, and $10,635,000.[55] Many of the person-

52. Elliff, *Reform of FBI Intelligence*, p. 57.

53. Sec. I of "Attorney General's Guidelines on Domestic Security Investigations," effective April 5, 1976, reprinted in House, Subcommittee on Civil Rights of the Judiciary Committee, *Hearings on FBI Oversight*, pp. 50-53.

54. GAO, *FBI Domestic Intelligence Operations: An Uncertain Future*, GGD-78-10, November 9, 1977, pp. 15-16.

55. House, Subcommittee on Civil Rights of the Judiciary Committee, *Hearings on FBI Oversight*, p. 42.

nel relieved were shifted to help carry the greatly increased workload created by the Freedom of Information Act and the Privacy Act. By March 1978, more than 6 percent of the FBI's total personnel were engaged in handling a veritable flood of requests for information.[56]

The 1976 guidelines have had only a limited effect on the investigation of foreign-directed subversive activities. The American Communist party (CPUSA), for example, has always been regarded as under the control of the Soviet Union, and it continues to be investigated under classified foreign counterintelligence guidelines, irrespective of the fact that it no longer presents a serious threat of violence or breaks a particular criminal statute. That is also true of Communist front organizations that have definite foreign ties. The situation gets murkier, however, when it comes to various New Left groups, many of which do not fit the neat separation between domestic and foreign-directed subversion.

How to draw this distinction was one of the issues raised in the trial in 1980 of two high-ranking FBI officials, W. Mark Felt and Edward S. Miller, who were found guilty of conspiring to violate the civil rights of relatives and friends of the radical Weather Underground by authorizing surreptitious entry into their homes in 1972 and 1973. Since early 1970 the Weather Underground had been engaged in a systematic campaign of bombing government buildings, including the Capitol and the Pentagon, police stations, banks, and corporate headquarters. It surfaced most recently again in a bungled holdup of a bank in New York state on October 20, 1981, which left two Nyack police officers and a Brinks security guard dead. Despite evidence that members of the Weather Underground had traveled frequently to Cuba, North Vietnam, and Eastern Europe, the prosecution in the Felt-Miller trial successfully rebutted the presence of "a significant foreign connection," the essential condition for a warrantless search in a security situation under the ruling of the Supreme Court in the so-called Keith case.[57] The Court in that case had acknowledged the difficulty of distinguishing between "domestic" and "foreign" unlawful activities directed against the U.S. government. That difficulty is still greater in instances of subversion that stay clear of illegal conduct.

It is arguable that during the 1950s and 1960s the FBI had indeed spread itself too thin and that Hoover's rigid (some call it morbid) preoccupation with the threat of domestic Communism had led the bureau to sweep with a broom that was far too broad. Tempted to

56. Testimony of the Department of Justice during Senate, Subcommittee on Criminal Laws of the Committee on the Judiciary, *Hearings on Erosion of Law Enforcement Intelligence*, p. 18, n. 33.

57. U.S. v. U.S. District Court, 407 U.S. 297 (1972).

accumulate a high caseload, the bureau collected much useless information unrelated to any criminal conduct as well as of doubtful utility for the loyalty-security program. We may now, however, have gone to the other extreme. At issue here is not only the drastic decline in the number of domestic intelligence investigations, discussed earlier, but also various restrictions on the indexing and keeping of records.

The FBI is subject to the same constraints of the Privacy Act as is the OPM; that is, since 1974 the bureau must publish in the *Federal Register* its systems of records on individuals, and it may not maintain records describing how individuals exercise rights guaranteed by the First Amendment unless expressly authorized by statute or by the individual concerned or as part of an authorized law enforcement activity. The FBI and the Department of Justice have taken the position that "authorized law enforcement activity" pertains to authorized investigations of organizations, but not to the investigation of individual members or associates of the organization. At the same time, once an organization is under investigation, it is then possible to compile information on individual members as well.

Some of the FBI's indexing aids have not fared so well. Several of these—like the rabble rouser index created in 1967 as an investigative aid to follow the activities of extremists traveling around the country encouraging violence—were phased out as no longer necessary even before the enactment of the Privacy Act.[58] Others, like the administrative index, became a casualty of the Privacy Act and of political pressures generated in the 1970s against FBI record keeping. The administrative index developed from the security index, which the FBI established in response to enactment of the Emergency Detention Act (Title II of the Internal Security Act of 1950).[59] That act required the detention during wartime or other declared emergency of persons considered dangerous to the security of the United States. At the time of the act's repeal in 1971,[60] the security index had about 12,000 names. The Justice Department concluded that the FBI's authority to investigate subversive activities was unaffected by the repeal of the Emergency Detention Act, and the index was reconstituted as an administrative index, albeit with much tighter standards. It now included only the leaders of subversive or extremist organizations and individuals who were known to be violence-prone—a total of about 1,250 persons. But even an investigative tool of such limited reach was

58. For a listing and description of the deactivated indexes, see GAO, *FBI Taking Actions to Comply Fully with the Privacy Act*, GGD-77-93, December 26, 1977, app. III.

59. 64 Stat. 1019, 50 U.S.C. 801.

60. Public Law 92-128, 85 Stat. 348.

no longer acceptable. The administrative index was abolished in January 1976 and put in storage on computer tape.[61]

Another instance when both the Department of Justice and the FBI gave ground to anti-intelligence sentiment in the country concerned a restrictive interpretation of the Levi guidelines with regard to the collection of publicly available information. The Justice Department took the position that unless the FBI was authorized to investigate an organization, it could not read, collect, or clip articles from the publications of such a group—publications that any other citizen in the country could read and use to form his opinion about the group's political aims. President Reagan's EO 12333 of December 4, 1981, "United States Intelligence Activities," authorizes the agencies concerned with foreign intelligence to collect "information that is publicly available,"[62] and it is to be hoped that the Justice Department will now abandon this particularly inane example of legalistic reasoning.

The FBI data base is also affected negatively by the bureau's policy, adopted in February 1973, of including in the national index of arrest information only arrests for serious crimes such as murder, robbery, and rape. Information on arrests for nonserious law violations such as vagrancy or drunkenness is no longer kept or disseminated, nor are arrest data on juveniles, which are disregarded unless the juvenile is treated and tried as an adult. It is also well to remember that there is no federal legislative mandate that would require state and local law enforcement agencies to submit arrest information to the FBI. In 1968, for example, the District of Columbia adopted the so-called Duncan ordinance, which forbade routine dissemination of arrest data by the Metropolitan Police Department. As a result of a court decision in 1975, the FBI had to purge approximately 91,000 District of Columbia arrest records from its files.[63]

In sum, then, it would appear that the FBI no longer has an adequate data base for the loyalty-security program. Government agencies have taken note of this situation and have largely ceased referring loyalty inquiries to the FBI. Between 1956 and 1970, the FBI investigated more than 10,000 appointees and 2,564 applicants on grounds of questionable loyalty.[64] In fiscal year 1973, the FBI opened 1,200 loyalty investigations on the basis of derogatory information

61. GAO, *FBI Taking Actions*, p. 33.

62. Sec. 2.3 of EO 12333, 46 F.R. 59941.

63. FBI testimony before House, Permanent Select Committee on Intelligence, *Hearings on Pre-Employment Security*, pp. 209-10.

64. Testimony of Kimbell Johnson, director of CSC Bureau of Personnel Investigations, on September 30, 1970, at House, Committee on Internal Security, *Hearings Regarding the Subversive Activities Control Act*, p. 5248.

discovered during the National Agency Check with Inquiries and 191 as a result of referral by other agencies. By fiscal year 1978 the total number of full field investigations for reasons of questionable loyalty was down to 40; in fiscal year 1981 it was 5.[65] For all practical purposes, the FBI today is out of the business of conducting loyalty investigations.

A definite contradiction exists today between the requirement of EO 10450 that the FBI provide information on membership in and the significance of subversive associations and the 1976 guidelines on domestic security investigations that forbid the collection of such information unless there is evidence of the use of violence or other illegal conduct. Groups that proclaim plans for revolution and for the infiltration of the armed forces—the Maoist Progressive Labor Party, for example—are no longer the subject of FBI monitoring unless they are also involved in some violation of federal law. The FBI closed its investigation of the Progressive Labor Party in September 1976. FBI official Paul Nugent, who testified before Congress in 1979 and who was asked whether the FBI would discover membership in the Progressive Labor Party as part of its National Agency Check (NAC), replied:

> I would say that the possibilities of our coming up with that name in a name check situation would be practically remote. . . . we just wouldn't have the currency of information with respect to that organization which has been closed now for 3 years. The membership of that particular group and any other could have changed two times in that period of 3 years, and we wouldn't have the identities of the membership.[66]

EO 10450 requires a full field investigation of anyone whose loyalty is in doubt; but, of course, unless the FBI has a warning signal in its intelligence collage, an agency in this kind of case would get a "No record" reply to its request for an NAC, and there would be no full field investigation.

The FBI is supposed to provide information on the character of organizations about which questions arise during personnel investigations. The Defense Investigative Service, for example, requires that in security investigations aimed at ascertaining the extent and significance of a subject's association with a questionable organization, the

65. Information provided by Loyalty and Applicants Section, Criminal Investigative Division, FBI.

66. FBI testimony at House, Permanent Select Committee on Intelligence, *Hearings on Pre-Employment Security*, p. 208.

FBI be asked for a "characterization of the organization."[67] Apart, however, from organizations clearly linked to a foreign power or those engaging in violence or some other illegal activity, the FBI no longer has up-to-date information on subversive organizations. Mere advocacy of revolution or revolutionary rhetoric, without a likelihood of some specific criminal activity, is not a sufficient basis for initiating a preliminary investigation of such groups because such utterances are regarded as protected by the First Amendment. FBI officials expressed the view to this author that such cases are handled flexibly and that anyone supporting the cause of violent revolution may find himself under investigation. This leaves a lot of uncovered ground. In a recently settled suit brought by the Alliance to End Repression and the American Civil Liberties Union against the FBI and CIA, the FBI agreed that in future domestic security investigations and inquiries it would be concerned only with criminal conduct and would not investigate any of the plaintiffs' activities protected by the First Amendment.[68] Therefore, government agencies that rely upon the FBI to keep them informed on the ever-changing radical and extremist scene will do so at their peril. An association with such groups may well turn out irrelevant in the case of most federal job applicants. Agencies should, however, know of such associations before they clear such persons for access to classified information or assign them to positions of trust and responsibility.

One consequence of the FBI charter legislation that was discussed by Congress in 1978 but never enacted would have been the transfer of responsibility for loyalty investigations from the FBI to OPM. The most important question here, however, is not who conducts such investigations but how one can run a functioning loyalty-security program without a suitable data base. Both OPM and FBI officials agree that this data base has been badly eroded and that something should be done to correct this situation. There also is general agreement that the initiative for this "something" will have to come from Congress. In the past, the FBI relied upon vague presidential directives and was left holding the bag when things went wrong. This will not happen again. Today the FBI sticks to the letter of the law. Congress, FBI officials argue, should tell them what kind of subversive organizations they

67. Defense Investigative Service, *Manual for Personnel Security Investigations,* DISM 20-1, January 30, 1981, p. 4-14.

68. Memorandum decision and order, Nos. 74C3268 and 75C3295, issued by U.S. district court judge Susan Getzendammer in Chicago on August 11, 1981. See Larry Williams, "Chicago Civil Rights Cases Settled," American Bar Association Standing Committee on Law and National Security, *Intelligence Report,* vol. 3, no. 9 (September 1981), p. 8.

want to see investigated and what kinds of records they want to have kept. At this writing, there is no indication that Congress is eager to do this.

It is worth noting that in the light of recent court rulings on the gathering of political intelligence, the FBI would appear to have considerable discretion. In 1971, a federal district court rejected a suit brought against the taking of pictures by local police officers at a demonstration. The mere existence of a chilling effect, said the court, was not decisive. The leaders of the demonstration had invited media coverage. "They invited the publicity and must stand the consequences."[69] A federal court of appeals confirmed this ruling. A year later, in *Laird* v. *Tatum*, the Supreme Court upheld the right of army intelligence and related civilian investigative agencies to collect information about public activities that had a potential for civil disorder. There was no evidence in this case, noted the Court, of any illegal or clandestine surveillance. The information gathered was nothing more than what a good newspaper reporter would have been able to obtain by attending public meetings and clipping articles from publications available on any newsstand. There was no showing of harm or threat of a specific future harm. Respondents simply "disagreed with the judgments made by the Executive Branch with respect to the type and amount of information the Army needs and [claimed] that the very existence of the Army's data-gathering system produces a constitutionally impermissible chilling effect upon the exercise of their First Amendment rights." To resolve this question of public policy, the Court concluded, may be an appropriate role for Congress; "it is not the role of the judiciary, absent actual present or immediately threatened injury resulting from unlawful governmental action."[70]

In another case, involving the Trotskyist Socialist Workers Party (SWP) and decided in 1974, the Supreme Court vacated an injunction that would have barred the attendance of FBI informants at the annual convention of the party's youth organization, the Young Socialist Alliance (YSA). The Court noted that the convention was open to the public and that any chilling effect caused by the attendance of the FBI informants, who were members of the organization, was not sufficient to outweigh the serious prejudice to the government of permanently compromising some or all of its informants in the organization. Governmental surveillance and infiltration that may dampen the exercise of First Amendment rights, Justice Marshall conceded, cannot be taken lightly. "But our abhorrence for abuse of governmental investi-

69. Donohue v. Duling, 330 F. Supp. 308, 310 (1971).
70. Laird v. Tatum, 408 U.S. 1, 13, and 15 (1972).

gative authority cannot be permitted to lead to an indiscriminate willingness to enjoin undercover investigation of any nature, whenever a countervailing First Amendment claim is raised."[71] The Supreme Court agreed with the lower courts that the great importance of preserving freedom of association justified barring the FBI, pending final resolution of the contested issues in the case, from transmitting the names of persons attending the convention to the CSC.

The FBI closed its investigation of the SWP in September 1976, but a lawsuit filed by the party in 1973, charging harassment and disruption of legal political activities, is only now coming to trial. The government has argued that the investigation of a party that included a faction favoring violence was a proper domestic security investigation under then existing guidelines. Moreover, and perhaps reflecting a new approach to domestic security by the Reagan administration, government lawyers have rejected an exclusive reliance upon the criminal activity yardstick required by the Levi guidelines:

> The issue in this case is not whether the Socialist Workers Party, the Young Socialist Alliance or any of their members can be proved guilty of a crime beyond a reasonable doubt. The issue is whether the government has a right to keep itself informed of the activities of groups that openly advocate revolutionary change in the structure and leadership of the government of the United States, even if such advocacy might be within the letter of the law.[72]

A rival and more militant Trotskyist group, the Spartacists, has ridiculed the attempt of the SWP to prove "that they are peaceful, legal parlor pinks and no threat to the U.S bourgeoisie"; unconditional defense of the Soviet Union against imperialist powers, the Spartacists maintained, has always been part of the ABC of Trotskyism.[73] Leaving aside the question of whether the SWP is or is not committed to violence and whether in case of war with the Soviet Union it might side with the country's enemy, the Justice Department apparently seeks to use this suit in order to establish once again the right of the FBI to conduct domestic security investigations even in the absence of specific illegal conduct.

One of the questions the courts will have to face in deciding this issue will be how to reconcile such investigations with the restrictive

71. Socialist Workers Party v. Attorney General of the United States, 419 U.S. 1314, 1319 (1974).

72. From a defense document quoted in Arnold H. Lubasch, "Marxist Group Charges Conspiracy as $40 Million Suit Goes to Trial," *New York Times*, April 4, 1981.

73. *Workers Vanguard*, April 10, 1981, p. 3.

provisions of the Privacy Act. There also is the question of the proper scope of such intelligence gathering. Even if one grants that the concept of total privacy is unrealistic and that political intelligence will necessarily brush against First Amendment rights of citizens, there remains the problem of setting the limits of such activities. Once the illegal activity yardstick is abandoned and especially if the prevention of infiltration of the government by members of extremist and subversive groups is once again accepted as a basis for FBI domestic security investigations, some other criteria will have to be found to define the range of these investigations.

It is arguable that in the past the FBI, often in collaboration with local "Red Squads," engaged in surveillance that was far too broad and was often useless for any valid intelligence purpose. The first successful lawsuit to force the release of such files ended in December 1980 in Detroit, and similar suits are pending in New York City, Seattle, Chicago, and Los Angeles.[74] Even before the outcome of this suit, many law enforcement agencies at state and local levels had abandoned such surveillance, had terminated their domestic intelligence squads, and had destroyed many of their files on extremists of the Left and Right. We face here again, however, the danger of throwing out the baby with the bath water. In guarding against abuses, one must not lose sight of the real threats of subversion that continue to exist.

It also would be wrong to impose civil or criminal liability for actions considered acceptable in a different legal and political climate. The conviction of FBI officials W. Mark Felt and Edward S. Miller in 1980 is said to have had a highly damaging impact on FBI morale, an effect not entirely erased by President Reagan's subsequent issue of a "full and unconditional" pardon on March 26, 1981. Meanwhile, more suits are pending for damages allegedly caused by undercover surveillance of activities protected by the First Amendment and improper investigative techniques. In December 1981, a federal jury awarded a total of $711,000 to seven former antiwar and civil rights activists and organizations, including $93,000 each to Arthur Waskow of the Institute for Policy Studies and the Washington Peace Center. The defendants were present or retired FBI officials and members of the Washington Metropolitan Police.[75] It remains to be seen whether the effort of the Reagan administration to rebuild the effectiveness of the intelligence services will include a restoration of the legitimate domestic security role of the FBI. The needs of the loyalty-security program, if nothing else, will demand no less.

74. Reginald Stuart, "Michigan to Release Its Files about Political Surveillance," *New York Times*, December 27, 1980.

75. Ben A. Franklin, "Ex-Activists Win $711,000 in 'Red Squads' Case," *New York Times*, December 24, 1981.

5
Problems of Staff

Funding and Size

Personnel security policy, most people would agree, should be developed in response to the requirements of security, and funds should be appropriated to do the job that needs to be done. Yet in the real world of government decision making it is often the other way around—fiscal constraints dictate policy. In the case of the loyalty-security program, this way of charting a course not only has not saved any money but in some instances has cost the government many additional millions of dollars. Shortages of investigative staff have led to delays in clearance that have become extremely costly and at the same time have increased the threat of compromising important national security information.

For a time, the problem was especially acute for the Defense Investigative Service (DIS), which handles the screening of DOD civilian and military personnel as well as industrial contractor employees. In 1980, 66 percent of the DIS investigative workload consisted of military personnel, a result in part of the considerable personnel turnover in the military. In all, DIS conducted in 1980 approximately 950,000 personnel security investigations. Of this total, about 800,000 were National Agency Checks (NACs), and the remaining 150,000 were Background Investigations (BIs) of various types. The DIS workload has increased substantially over the years—about 18 percent between 1978 and 1980 alone—but the agency had been getting less and less money with which to provide services. In 1975, as a result of cuts directed by the House Appropriations Committee, DIS funding was reduced by 25 percent. By 1980, the total cut in resources was 40 percent. The result was a drastic increase in the average time required to process clearance requests and the accumulation of a substantial case backlog.[1]

1. Figures are taken from U.S. Congress, House, Subcommittee on Oversight of the Select Committee on Intelligence, *Hearings on Pre-Employment Security Procedures of the Intelligence Agencies*, 96th Cong., 1st sess., May 16-June 21, 1979, pp. 70-74; U.S. Congress, House, Subcommittee on Investigations of the Committee on Post Office and

The consequences of these cuts in funding can be seen in the increase of the average number of days to process BIs and NACs conducted by the DIS for industrial contractors:

Fiscal Year	BIs	NACs
1978	96	46
1979	104	57
1980	136	68
1981 (May 31, 1981)	220	103

The General Accounting Office (GAO), which compiled these figures, noted that the delays in processing requests for security clearance increase costs to the government, result in delays in contract completion, and increase the risks to national security. In a memorandum to the secretary of defense dated July 21, 1981, the deputy under secretary of defense for policy referred to the effect of the delays as follows: "This inordinate delay in finalizing security clearances results in large numbers of personnel who cannot be productively utilized for extended periods, costly slippage in initiation or schedules of classified contracts, and some degradation of operational readiness."[2] A 1977 study made by industry estimated an average loss of about $31 a day for each employee unable to work on the classified portion of a government contract and therefore working at less than his full productivity. Adjusting for inflation, GAO estimated that delays in processing could cost the government $580 million in 1982.[3]

In addition to significant losses in productivity, delays in processing have increased threats to the national security. Because of the urgency of some defense programs and the extensive delays in obtaining clearances, the Defense Industrial Security Clearance Office (DISCO) has been granting an increasing number of interim SECRET and TOP SECRET clearances to contractor personnel:[4]

Fiscal Year	Interim Clearances Issued
1978	6,136
1979	6,831
1980	9,567
1981 (estimate)	11,350

Civil Service, *Hearing on Federal Personnel Background Investigations*, 96th Cong., 2d sess., March 25, 1980, pp. 16-22; U.S. General Accounting Office (GAO), *Faster Processing of DOD Personnel Security Clearances Could Avoid Millions in Losses*, GGD-81-105, September 15, 1981.

2. GAO, *Faster Processing*, pp. 6-7.

3. Ibid., p. 8.

4. Ibid., p. 9.

No figures are available on how many of these interim clearances were later revoked because of derogatory information discovered during the investigations subsequently conducted, but there is no reason to assume that the number of denials in these cases would differ from the usual ratio of denials, which has been running at 0.4 percent during the years in question.[5] This means that during 1980, for example, thirty-eight individuals whose clearance subsequently had to be revoked because of derogatory information may have received an interim clearance for SECRET or TOP SECRET information and started work on classified contracts. The consequence of this state of affairs for national security can only be guessed.

In January 1979, DIS had a backlog of 31,800 unprocessed cases of BIs; by March 1980, the backlog had grown to 47,800 cases. By the end of fiscal year 1982, the backlog was expected to reach 89,700 cases. In order to reduce these massive delays and bring the growing caseload under control, the deputy secretary of defense announced in June 1981 that, except for immigrant aliens, individuals would no longer receive a BI before being given access to SECRET information; a moratorium would be placed on all periodic reinvestigations, which generally are required every five years for individuals in critical-sensitive positions and for those with access to special program information; and a new Interview-oriented Background Investigation (IBI) would be used in place of the traditional BI.[6]

The first of these three actions ordered is not of any great moment, for few BIs had ever been conducted for these kinds of positions. There are some critics who think that more BIs *should* be used. At present, it is possible for a person to be accepted into the armed forces on the basis of an Entrance National Agency Check (ENTNAC), which is an NAC without a fingerprint check. Recruiting commands are expected to supplement the NAC with inquiries to schools and local law enforcement agencies, but, for reasons discussed in the previous chapter, the results of these inquiries are often meager. On the basis of this limited screening the enlistee is given access to information and technology up to the level of SECRET. An enlistee could, for example, end up on a nuclear submarine or be in contact with important classified information or computer data. Members of the armed forces, it is argued by some security officers, live in a controlled environment and are under fairly constant supervision, but whether this fact is sufficient to make up for the rather loose initial screening is open to question. During the ten-year period 1972–1981, the army, for example, procured over 1½ million first enlistments. No data are available on how

5. Figures provided by DIS Office of Information and Legal Affairs.
6. GAO, *Faster Processing,* p. 14.

many enlistments were denied on loyalty-security grounds. We do know that during these ten years only twenty-eight enlisted members were separated for security reasons—reasons that, in addition to questionable political associations, include relatives behind the Iron Curtain or recurring financial difficulties.[7] It would appear to be fair to conclude that the armed forces do not now have an effective program to screen out individuals of questionable loyalty and to preclude their access to several types of classified information.

The moratorium on reinvestigation is another potential danger to national security. DOD officials maintain that military superiors are under instructions to know their people and to be alert for situations that require special security attention. The majority of adverse security actions are said to be based on information coming from sources other than BIs.[8] Yet these reinvestigations at times do lead to revocations of clearance and therefore are not simply dispensable.

Some long-time personnel security officials are skeptical also about the new type of BI that is now in use. The new IBI procedure stresses the importance of an initial subject interview, which, it is said, can clear up many issues before numerous man-hours are invested in their resolution by way of an expensive field investigation. DOD officials maintain that they adopted the IBI not to save money but to improve efficiency after a pilot study published in March 1981, which indicated that the IBI developed three times as much significant information as the traditional BI. But not everyone accepts the validity of these findings. OPM officials point out that the IBI covers far less ground than the BI—there is no check with employers, educational institutions, or references. There is the danger, it is argued, that the subject in such an interview can, through partial admissions, divert attention from significant and damaging information and may succeed in directing the inquiry through leads provided by him.[9] As a result of OPM objections, DOD reinstituted the traditional BI for its civilian employees.

The GAO has argued that the only immediate relief measure for

7. Communication from the Office of the Deputy Chief of Staff for Personnel, U.S. Army, March 10, 1982.

8. See House, Subcommittee on Oversight of the Select Committee on Intelligence, *Hearings on Pre-Employment Security*, p. 59.

9. The IBI is described in DIS, *Procedures to Implement an Interview-oriented BI*, June 26, 1981. For a critique see David Martin, "The Erosion of the Federal Employee Security Program: A Critique," unpublished manuscript, December 1981, pp. 62-63. Critical comments on this type of investigation can also be found in White House Domestic Counsel Committee on the Right to Privacy, Project no. 10, *A Study Conducted by the Task Force on Personnel Investigations and Adjudications*, February 1975, II, p. 72.

the problems that have arisen is to hire a substantial number of additional investigators. In fiscal year 1981, the DIS had 1,071 authorized investigators, of whom 996 were actually assigned. In May 1981, the director of DIS estimated that in order to reduce turnaround time for investigations to sixty-five days by the end of fiscal year 1982, assuming that requests increased at the same rate they had over the past three years, DIS would require 880 additional positions (investigators and support staff).[10] Since this recommendation for a greatly augmented staff was made, the DIS has received 768 additional positions, some of them filled with OPM and retired federal investigators. These remedial actions should have an appreciable effect.

Another source of delays for security clearance is the excessively long turnaround time for NACs in the FBI Identification Division, a procedure designed to screen out those with a criminal record. When the division receives a request for a fingerprint identification, the staff searches the FBI criminal file that contains arrest records and related fingerprint cards by comparing the name and other descriptive items on the request with data in the files. If there is a tentative match with an arrest record on file, the incoming fingerprint card is compared with the card on file. If the name search is unsuccessful, the time-consuming manual process of trying to match the incoming fingerprint card with fingerprint cards in the file must be carried out. During the 1960s, the average time to process requests was three workdays. By 1980, the turnaround time was twenty-six workdays, and there was a backlog of 564,000 fingerprint cards. The average time for processing DOD requests was fifty-eight calendar days in June 1981.[11]

The FBI has attributed the increase in turnaround time to three factors: the growth in the size of the files, the difficulty of recruiting and retaining a sufficient number of qualified personnel, and substantial new processing burdens resulting from privacy legislation, regulations, and court decisions. While the burden of service has increased, the personnel of the Identification Division has been substantially reduced. In fiscal year 1979, the division had an authorized staff of 3,620; by fiscal year 1981, that number was down to 2,863. The FBI estimates that, without a backlog, a staff of about 3,600 could respond to requests in a turnaround time of about ten workdays. The delays in processing have also had a damaging effect on the entire criminal justice system by impeding criminal investigations and hampering prosecutorial, penal, and parole actions.

10. GAO, *Faster Processing*, pp. 10-11.
11. Ibid., pp. 11-12.

On October 1, 1981, as a short-term remedy for one year, the FBI suspended making fingerprint checks for banks and state and local authorities, other than criminal justice agencies, submitted for employment and licensing purposes. By January 12, 1982, this action had succeeded in reducing the backlog of cases to 245,631 and shortening the response time to 19.6 workdays.[12] The long-term solution to the increasing workload and backlog is automation, which is under way but is costly. Such an automated system would be substantially more accurate than the existing manual system and could have a response time of eight hours, including incoming and outgoing time in the mailroom.[13] Also needed is a more reliable system of taking fingerprints. In fiscal year 1976, 27 percent of all requests involved prints that were not classifiable or had other missing information.[14]

As discussed earlier in this chapter, background investigations (BIs) take even longer than NACs and NACIs. In order not to lose a desirable employee to another organization or agency with less stringent hiring criteria, many agencies therefore routinely conduct BIs on a "postemployment" basis. A GAO survey of applicants to critical-sensitive positions, carried out in 1974, found in 62 percent of the cases reviewed that individuals had been hired before their BIs had been completed.[15] Another survey, by OPM and covering a sample period of forty-five days in 1980, revealed that in many departments the percentage of persons appointed to critical-sensitive positions before completion of their BIs ranged between 90 and 100 percent.[16] OPM data confirmed what security officers have known for a long time—that the rate of favorable determinations in postappointment investigations is double that of preappointment investigations. Once on the job, friendly personal relations quickly develop, which militate against a dismissal even in the face of derogatory information discovered during the BI. These practices have obvious implications for national security and are in direct violation of Section 3(b) of EO 10450, which allows the filling of a sensitive position before completion of a full field investigation only in a case of emergency.

12. Letter of February 23, 1982, to author by deputy assistant director (operations) of Identification Division, FBI.

13. GAO, *Faster Processing*, pp. 16-17; "Fingerprint ID's Cut Back by FBI," *New York Times*, October 13, 1981.

14. GAO, *Proposals to Resolve Longstanding Problems in Investigations of Federal Employees*, FPCD-77-64, December 16, 1977, p. 30.

15. GAO, *Personnel Security Investigations: Inconsistent Standards and Procedures*, B-132376, December 2, 1974, p. 10.

16. OPM, *Office of Internal Evaluation, Personnel Investigations: Ways to Improve and Reduce Costs*, September 1980, p. 12.

The Qualifications of Investigators

"For forms of government let fools contest; whate'er is best administer'd is best," wrote Alexander Pope in his *Essay on Man*. One is tempted to paraphrase and apply this saying to the different security systems in existence. There is much impressionistic evidence to indicate that the effectiveness of such programs depends to a great degree on the qualifications of their staff, adjudicators and investigators alike.

"Almost all of the excesses of the loyalty and security programs are attributable to the incredible political ignorance and naiveté of the personnel of the Review Boards," wrote Sidney Hook, a critic interested in a more effective security program, in 1959.[17] Even though officials dealing with security issues were supposed to have a good knowledge of current affairs and national security problems as well as "a general knowledge of subversive organizations and their methods of operation,"[18] in practice these officials often had great difficulty telling a Communist from a socialist or a liberal. What held true for members of review boards and for departmental security officers was even more of a problem for the investigators doing the actual work in the field. It was difficult to recruit competent persons for these assignments. CSC Chairman Phillip Young testified before Congress in 1955 that 50 percent of the candidates for the job of investigator failed the written examination, and of those passing that test 50 percent failed the oral examination.[19]

Official interest in providing security personnel with some knowledge about the radical political scene of the day continued until the early 1970s. CSC General Counsel Anthony L. Mondello told the House Internal Security Committee in 1972:

> The Commission thoroughly trains its own investigators and adjudicators with respect to subversive ideologies. We are aware that the major agencies conduct similar training. . . . Because of the rather abrupt changes in the kind of violent action organizations over the past 5 years, courses dealing with the strategy and tactics of Soviet Communism are not

17. Sidney Hook, *Political Power and Personal Freedom: Critical Studies in Democracy, Communism and Civil Rights* (New York: Collier Books, 1959), p. 248.

18. CSC Circular no. 743, February 24, 1954, "Qualifications Standards for Personnel Security Officer Positions," reprinted in U.S. Congress, Senate, Committee on Post Office and Civil Service, *Hearings on the Administration of the Federal Employees Security Program*, part 1, 84th Cong., 1st sess., 1955, p. 64.

19. Ralph S. Brown, Jr., *Loyalty and Security: Employment Tests in the United States* (New Haven, Conn.: Yale University Press, 1958), p. 28, n. 12.

broad enough to meet current needs.[20]

No information is available on how effective this training was. What-ever the benefits of this instruction, however, none of it survived the abolition of the attorney general's list and the changed political climate of the post-Watergate period. Neither OPM nor DIS any longer has such political training. OPM's current tests for applicants are limited to ascertaining general competence in responding to hypothetical situa-tions encountered by investigators; there is no reference to current affairs. As one OPM official put it to this author: "What's the use of training people in problems of loyalty and subversion if you cannot use such criteria anyway?"

The old problem of attracting persons of adequate caliber has continued to this day. Candidates are hired at the GS-5 level, with a 1981 salary of $12,854 per year. They must have three years' exper-ience of administrative or other work that provides evidence of the ability to perform the duties of investigator. Unpaid volunteer work or college education may be substituted for job experience.[21] To qualify for these positions a person need not have had a college education; many of the better-qualified candidates use these jobs as a stepping stone to other government positions. "Speaking quite frankly," the associate director of OPM's Staffing Services Group told a congres-sional committee in 1980, "investigative positions, while we think they require a high order of skill to perform a very valuable service, are not the kinds of positions that appeal to a lot of prospective candi-dates. And so trying to find good quality candidates who can do the kind of work with the level of proficiency that we require is a very, very demanding job."[22] OPM currently has under development a career retention plan to enhance the attractiveness of investigative positions, but the results of this effort remain to be seen.

OPM investigators are not well paid, and little prestige is derived from these jobs. In contrast to the FBI special agents, no glamour is attached to the position of OPM investigator, and morale is said to be low. In addition to these problems of long standing, if a working loyalty program were to be reestablished, all agencies would face the problem of rebuilding expertise in this area, which by now has largely been lost. Many of the older officials, with political experience devel-

20. U.S. Congress, House, Committee on Internal Security, *Hearings Regarding the Administration of the Subversive Activities Control Act of 1950 and the Federal Civilian Em-ployee Loyalty-Security Program*, part 4, 92d Cong., 2d sess., 1972, pp. 5886-87.

21. Cf. OPM, Personnel Investigations Program, *Investigator: A Critical Mission, a Career with a Future (1980)*.

22. Testimony of Arch S. Ramsay before House, Subcommittee on Investigations of the Post Office and Civil Service Committee, *Hearing on Federal Personnel Security*, p. 32.

oped in the 1950s and 1960s, have retired. Newer employees lack both the requisite education and training and, given the disuse of loyalty criteria during the last fifteen years or so, have hardly any experience in the field of subversion.

Writing of the men who administered the loyalty program of the 1950s, Sidney Hook noted that to many of these people "Communist language was gobbledegook, Communist ideas suspiciously like the ideas of socialists, dogooders and even New Dealers, and Communist organizations with the distinctions between member, sympathizer, front, dupe, innocent, and honest mistaken liberal, as mysterious as the order of being in the science of angelology."[23] Today, the radical scene is far more complex than it ever was in the 1950s. Both the Old and the New Left are split into numerous organizations, and to evaluate the significance of organizational ties now has become an even more challenging assignment. Well-meaning but politically unsophisticated investigators and adjudicators face this chaotic scene without any central guidance or political training and without workable criteria of loyalty and subversion. One can only hope that some day we will not have to pay a high price for this accumulation of neglect.

23. Hook, *Political Power*, p. 248.

6
Conclusions and Recommendations

The problems that have developed in the loyalty-security program run deep, beyond the intentions of specific individuals. Nobody can know how many persons by now have taken advantage of the virtual collapse of the loyalty provisions of the program. What can and must be said is that today we no longer have adequate means to keep subversive elements out of public employment. Absolute security, as Justice Holmes observed in another connection, is achieved only in the graveyard. Yet at the present time we no longer enjoy even a modest assurance of more limited security. The shortcomings in the program are serious, and the need for reform is urgent. Such reforms could be made without jeopardizing important individual liberties.

The difficulty in achieving changes in a program that has been muddling along since 1953 should not be underestimated. Time and again during the last thirty years study commissions have pointed out various problems in the loyalty-security program and have urged reform. In 1956 there was the report of the Special Committee of the Association of the Bar of the City of New York, chaired by Dudley B. Bonsal.[1] In 1955 Congress authorized the establishment of a bipartisan commission on government security. The report of this commission, chaired by Lloyd Wright, a former president of the American Bar Association, was published in 1957.[2] More recently, in 1975, a government task force chaired by David O. Cooke, then as now deputy assistant secretary of defense for administration, conducted Project 10, a review of the loyalty-security program.[3] None of the proposals for reform emanating from these commissions of inquiry have been implemented, and there can be little doubt that to this day the entire

1. *Report of the Special Committee on the Federal Loyalty-Security Program of the Association of the Bar of the City of New York* (New York: Dodd, Mead, 1956).

2. *Report of the Commission on Government Security* (Washington, D.C., 1957).

3. White House Domestic Council Committee on the Right to Privacy, Project no. 10, *A Study Conducted by the Task Force on Personnel Investigations and Adjudications* (Washington, D.C., 1975).

issue of loyalty and subversion remains highly sensitive and contro-
versial. For large segments of the intellectual community, the abuses
revealed in the programs of the 1940s and 1950s have discredited the
idea of any kind of loyalty-security program; some of them have called
for the abolition of a system characterized by "fundamental senseless-
ness."[4] Many conservatives are aware of the serious problems that
have developed over the years, but they are unable to agree on an
alternative program. As of this writing, the Reagan administration,
too, has other priorities and appears unwilling to spend political cap-
ital on an issue that is sure to give rise to an emotional and divisive
public debate.

One would like to hope against hope that it will not take another
Alger Hiss case, the exposure of a traitor in high places, to create a
willingness to take remedial action. There is the danger that such a
scandal could lead to an overreaction as bad and dangerous for civil
liberties as was the McCarthyism of the 1950s. Be that as it may, and in
full awareness of the obstacles that face any attempt to reopen this
complex and contentious issue, this chapter is devoted to making
suggestions for changes in the loyalty-security program.

The implementation of several of these proposals will require
action by Congress, though constitutional considerations do not appear to be an issue. The duty of the government to protect itself against
subversion and to preserve the security of the American people has
been affirmed by the Supreme Court many times.[5] "The Court's day-
to-day task is to reject as false claims in the name of civil liberty which,
if granted, would paralyze or impair authority to defend existence of
our society, and to reject as false claims in the name of security which
would undermine our freedoms and open the way to oppression."[6]
Hence, the Constitution being the open-ended instrument of government it is, if a clear national need can be demonstrated, support for
such action can undoubtedly be discovered in the law of the land. The
courts will uphold legislation that addresses legitimate demands of
national security without unnecessarily trampling upon protected
liberties.

The recommendations that follow are listed in rough order of
importance.

1. Congress should amend the Privacy Act to allow the collection of infor-

4. This is the phrase of Philip M. Stern in the foreword to the M.I.T. edition of the
documents of the Oppenheimer case, *In the Matter of J. Robert Oppenheimer* (Cambridge,
Mass.: M.I.T. Press, 1971), p. xi.

5. See, for example, U.S. v. U.S. District Court, 407 U.S. 297, 310 (1972).

6. American Communications Association v. Douds, 339 U.S. 382, 445 (1950).

mation and the maintenance of records on organizations that aim at the destruction of the American constitutional system of government or deny its legitimacy. The repair of the data base of the loyalty-security program is probably the measure that has the greatest importance and urgency. According to the Levi guidelines of 1976, the FBI has authority to collect and maintain information on groups and individuals who engage in or plan to engage in illegal conduct such as overthrowing the government or depriving persons of their civil rights under the Constitution. This is inadequate.

The domestic intelligence data base should include information on Marxist-Leninist organizations that favor a radical restructuring of the American system of constitutional government, that is, abolition of the Bill of Rights, of provisions for the rule of law, and of periodic free elections with competing political candidates and parties. It also should include those groups of the New Left, descended from "The Movement" of the 1960s, that continue to struggle against what they call the "illegitimate authority" of the American government. Some of these organizations, like the Committees of Solidarity with the People of El Salvador and Nicaragua, have time-bound, limited objectives. Others, like the recently organized National Black Independent Political party, probably have no foreign ties, though their positions on key policy issues usually do not differ from those of the Soviet Union or Cuba. New Left groups that reject the basic equity and legitimacy of America's political and social institutions and seek to dismantle the "national security state" should be part of the domestic intelligence collage even if they lack the Old Left's clear programmatic commitments and irrespective of whether their advocacy of radical change is within the letter of the law. The purpose of this data base is to enable adjudicators of the loyalty-security program to evaluate the significance of organizational ties.

To the extent possible, and in line with the ruling of the Supreme Court in *Laird* v. *Tatum* discussed in chapter 4, the data on organizations should be gathered from publicly available sources such as publications and attendance at public meetings. This information should be collected, analyzed, and evaluated by a team of social scientists and lawyers working under the aegis of the Justice Department, similar to the work directed in 1940–1941 by Professor Harold Laswell of Yale University in implementation of Section 9-A of the Hatch Act and the Voorhis Anti-Propaganda Act.[7] In special cases where the attorney general has determined that publicly available sources are not sufficient for a full understanding of a group's aims and modes of oper-

7. Eleanor Bontecou, *The Federal Loyalty-Security Program* (Ithaca, N.Y.: Cornell University Press, 1953), pp. 164-65.

ation, the services of the FBI should be enlisted. In such cases, the least intrusive collection technique feasible should be used. Undisclosed participation in such organizations by anyone acting on behalf of the FBI should similarly be subject to approval by the director of the FBI and by the attorney general. These ground rules are already part of President Reagan's EO 12333 on U.S. intelligence activities, promulgated in December 1981.[8] Section 2.3(g) of that order permits the collection and retention of information "arising out of a lawful personnel, physical or communications security investigation." An explicit endorsement of this presidential directive will be necessary, however, since EO 12333 deals primarily with foreign intelligence and since the collection of information suggested here—even though in aid of personnel investigations—will involve not just applicants for public employment. Such legislation is also required in order to allow for the dissemination of this information to OPM and to other federal agencies in support of personnel background investigations and in order to eliminate any possible conflict with the Privacy Act.

The information on organizations should be regarded as intelligence data and should be kept confidential. It should not be another attorney general's list of subversive organizations. A formal public list would undoubtedly give rise to numerous lawsuits by organizations seeking to challenge their listing and could tie up the list in the courts for years to come. Members of such groups would be able to contest the correctness of the Justice Department's characterization of the organization to which they belong, or they could demonstrate that their membership is innocent if they are denied employment on account of such membership. An administrative hearing at that point, as Justice Jackson argued in his concurring opinion in the *Joint Anti-Fascist Refugee Committee* case discussed in chapter 4, would "be a permissible solution of a difficult problem" and would satisfy the requirements of due process of law.[9]

2. Congress should enact legislation that would mandate the use of loyalty criteria in personnel actions involving sensitive positions. Since 1968, no person has been denied employment or been dismissed from the federal government on grounds of disloyalty. Government officials entrusted with the administration of the loyalty-security program argue that court decisions and the Privacy Act prevent them from applying the loyalty criteria of EO 10450 and of applicable civil service suitability rules. Mere membership in the Communist party and other subversive organizations is held to be an activity protected by the First

8. EO 12333 of December 4, 1981, 46 F.R. 59941.
9. Joint Anti-Fascist Refugee Committee v. McGrath, 341 U.S. 123, 186 (1951).

Amendment and not a disqualification even for sensitive positions.

The legal reasoning in support of this argument is questionable. It is based on cases involving nonsensitive positions such as state public school teachers or resident physicians at VA hospitals. In order to counter such strained interpretations of the Constitution, Congress should make it clear that loyalty is a prerequisite for holding a sensitive position in the federal government. Not every person who is a security risk is disloyal, but every disloyal person is ipso facto a security risk.

While it may be neither easy nor advisable to legislate an operational definition of loyalty, it is possible to establish criteria for disloyalty. At the minimum, these should include (1) actively promoting the policy objectives of a Communist country for either monetary gain or ideological reasons, and (2) being actively opposed to the democratic form of government of this country and favoring a totalitarian system of rule. For a variety of reasons, a democratic society may decide to tolerate activities or beliefs of this kind, but, in Justice Vinson's felicitous phrase, there is no need to make a person committed to them the keeper of the arsenal. Organizational ties are relevant for assessing disloyalty. Membership in any of the many different Communist parties operating in the United States today or in certain New Left groups is not proof of disloyalty, but it raises a prima facie case of possible disloyalty that must be explored. The fact and significance of membership in such organizations should be ascertained during personnel background investigations through both written and oral interrogatories. The fact that these organizations are allowed to operate legally and that membership in them is protected by the First Amendment is irrelevant from the point of view of a personnel loyalty program. Disloyalty and criminality are not synonymous. The purpose of the loyalty-security program is not to punish crime but to prevent it and to safeguard the integrity of government personnel.

When writing this kind of legislation, great care will have to be taken to use precise language. The rule of law and elementary fairness demand that citizens know in advance what kinds of conduct or beliefs are considered disloyal by their government and will disqualify them for certain positions in public employment. At the same time, it must be remembered that the loyalty-security program cannot be held to the same standards of specificity that prevail in criminal proceedings. Criteria and guidelines for adjudicators must allow for flexibility in their application to individual cases. Each case must be weighed on its own merits, taking into consideration all relevant factors and prior experience in similar cases. Each adjudication must be a common-sense determination based upon an assessment of all available information, both favorable and unfavorable; it must seek to ascertain those past and present behavioral patterns that may reasonably be expected to continue in the future.

In the last analysis, adjudicators will have to make a judgment that is rationally related to the facts relied upon but that in the nature of the case cannot be absolutely certain and exact. The standard to be applied is the affirmative finding that clearance will be consistent with the demands of national security or the national interest. In some instances, as for example in the case of persons like Christopher Boyce who are deeply alienated from the American way of life without having joined subversive organizations or developed a coherent alternative ideology, adjudicators will have to rely on information developed through a rigorous personal interview that should be part of all clearance procedures for critical-sensitive positions. As the court decisions reviewed in chapter 3 have indicated, disqualification does not depend upon proof of criminal or disloyal conduct or of intent to engage in such activities. This is a heavy burden for adjudicators to carry. Much will depend upon their sound judgment, mature thinking, and careful analysis as well as the reliability of the information at their disposal. Neither guidelines nor legislation should be allowed to impose a straitjacket upon the deliberations of adjudicators, who must be held to the highest standards of performance.

3. The funding of the loyalty-security program should be increased so as to allow an expansion of the investigative staff and an upgrading of its caliber. Cuts in funding for DIS and the FBI during the 1970s have led to lengthy delays in clearance that have cost the government many millions of dollars in lost utilization of highly skilled personnel. At the same time, the increased resort to interim clearances has increased threats to the national security. Such shortsighted and counterproductive attempts to economize must not be repeated; investigative agencies should be funded at levels adequate for a timely delivery of their important services.

Equally, or perhaps even more, important would be a substantial improvement in the caliber of the investigative staff. A college degree should be required of all new employees. Special training courses to impart knowledge of subversive ideologies and organizations and their modes of operation should be restored. Since a high percentage of the adjudicative and administrative personnel of OPM and DIS are promoted to these positions from the ranks of the investigative staff, such upgrading will in the long run also improve the entire process of adjudication.

4. The loyalty provisions of the loyalty-security program should be limited to sensitive positions in the civilian civil service and to persons with access to information classified SECRET and TOP SECRET. All appointments to positions in the civilian sector of the federal government are theoretically subject to the clearance procedures of EO 10450 and to the requirement that all personnel be "of complete and unswerving loyalty to the United States." Similarly, civil service rules include as grounds for disqualification "reasonable doubt as to the loyalty of the person involved to the government of the United States." In practice, as we have seen, since 1968 no denials or dismissals have taken place on grounds of questionable loyalty or security. OPM and DIS investigators are under instructions to look into the loyalty of applicants, but in view of the confusion surrounding the concepts of loyalty and subversion and on account of the limits that have been placed on written and oral interrogatories, these inquiries are not very meaningful. In response to a report of the General Accounting Office critical of the CSC's loyalty standards and investigations, the executive director of the CSC, Raymond Jacobson, acknowledged on October 6, 1977: "We are in complete agreement with GAO's assessment of the futility of most so-called loyalty investigations."[10] All this has created a situation where the loyalty criteria of the clearance process are perceived by many as a veritable anachronism.

Debate over the scope of the loyalty-security program is of long standing. According to one school of thought, as expressed by a congressman some years ago, "no person who is not satisfied with our form of government should be permitted to draw compensation from that government."[11] This moral proposition, insisting on a loyalty test for all government jobs, is often linked to the more pragmatic argument that disloyal persons will seek to impede or to obstruct the successful operation of the government or in various devious ways will impair the morale of their fellow workers. The distinction between sensitive and nonsensitive positions is held to be unrealistic and impossible to draw in practice. The very presence of disloyal individuals in public employment, it is argued, will undermine the confidence and trust of the people in their government. This last argument carries considerable political weight. Few members of Congress will dare vote against legislation that bars subversive elements, no matter how loosely defined, from public employment. Legislation to endorse formally the current practice of accepting "mere members" of the Communist party into public employment would undoubtedly go down to a resounding defeat.

10. U.S. General Accounting Office (GAO), *Proposals to Resolve Longstanding Problems in Investigations of Federal Employees,* FPCD-77-64, December 16, 1977, p. 75.
11. Statement of Representative Nichols on July 20, 1939, quoted in David H. Rosenbloom, *Federal Service and the Constitution: The Development of the Public Employment Relationship* (Ithaca, N.Y.: Cornell University Press, 1971), p. 144.

Another school of thought concedes that the government, even more than most employers, is entitled to demand and receive the loyalty of those who serve it, but questions the need for a formal machinery to ensure that employees in nonsensitive positions are in fact loyal. A loyalty program for all government workers is held to be unnecessary, for if a disloyal person "is not in a position to influence policy, and has no access to classified materials, his opportunity to do harm is limited."[12] Government policy emerges with great difficulty from the strain of a hundred different pressures, and the opportunity for any one person to make or even influence policy, unless he is at the top of the bureaucratic hierarchy, is therefore limited.[13] Moreover, it is argued that whatever the benefits of such a program, one should take account of its costs and risks. In the words of Professor Walter Gellhorn:

> When a man's acts may heavily affect the community's safety, a judgment concerning his probable future conduct may appropriately be made, even though the judgment is perforce inexact. In such a case society balances risks. On the one hand there is a risk that infidelity may cause grievous injury to the nation. On the other hand there is a risk that an erroneous conclusion about an individual may be grievously injurious to him. It is not unreasonable to conclude that the first of these risks outweighs the second, and that personnel security determinations are therefore well justified. The justification, however, is related to and derives from the existence of potentially grave danger. If danger is in fact not present, or if its degree is inconsiderable, the stated justification vanishes.[14]

Those opposed to the use of loyalty tests for all positions argue that even such a sweeping program cannot guarantee total security. There is no absolute assurance against betrayal or espionage or sabotage. A more prudent course, they suggest, is to classify positions according to whether one or a few employees could cause ascertainable damage in them and to concentrate countermeasures upon those that are sensitive. Finite resources mean that in practice we have to choose between more effective protection for truly important positions and less effective protection for all. As the Harvard physicist

12. Ralph S. Brown, Jr., *Loyalty and Security: Employment Tests in the United States* (New Haven, Conn.: Yale University Press, 1958), p. 337.

13. Earl Latham, *The Communist Conspiracy in Washington: From the New Deal to McCarthy* (Cambridge, Mass.: Harvard University Press, 1966), p. 360.

14. Walter Gellhorn, *Security, Loyalty and Science* (Ithaca, N.Y.: Cornell University Press, 1950), p. 126.

Dean Van Vleck has put it: "The moment we start guarding our tooth-brushes and our diamond rings with equal zeal, we usually lose fewer toothbrushes but more diamond rings."[15]

In effect, then, this second school of thought argues for a security program to protect sensitive positions similar to that operating in Great Britain. For such sensitive positions, loyalty is a crucial qualifica-tion, but to attempt to screen out the disloyal from nonsensitive posi-tions is a wasted effort. An employee who fails to discharge the duties of his office, whether motivated by disloyalty or just plain incompe-tence, can and should of course be dismissed in any position. Even off-duty conduct may have to be considered. This kind of program does not, however, require a general screening for loyalty of all government workers.

The suggestion made here to limit the application of loyalty crite-ria to sensitive positions endorses the reasoning of the second of the two approaches described above. If implemented it would undercut the cynicism that has developed with regard to the loyalty aspects of the current program, and it would concentrate investigative resources where they are most needed. Also required is a better definition of what constitutes a sensitive position.

EO 10450 provides that the occupants of positions that would have a materially adverse effect on the national security be classified "sensitive." The order is not clear, however, as to what constitutes national security. The Supreme Court noted this problem in the 1956 case of *Cole* v. *Young*, decided three years after the promulgation of EO 10450, when it found that the removal authority of the order was applicable only to occupants of sensitive positions. The Court took the position that the term "national security," in the interests of which summary discharge was authorized by the Summary Suspension Act of 1950[16] (an authority extended by EO 10450 to all federal agencies), had reference only to those activities directly concerned with the na-tion's safety and not with the general welfare. It is clear from the face of the 1950 statute and its legislative history, said the Court, that "national security" was "intended to comprehend only those activi-ties of the government that are directly concerned with the protection of the Nation from internal subversion or foreign aggression"—activi-ties that entailed access to classified materials.[17] Sensitive positions, therefore, were only those positions that related to national security in this restricted sense of the term.

In 1965, after an internal review of EO 10450 endorsed by Presi-

15. Quoted in *Report of the Special Committee of the Bar of the City of New York,* p. 148.
16. Public Law 81-733 of August 26, 1950, 64 Stat. 476, 5 U.S.C. 7532.
17. Cole v. Young, 351 U.S. 536, 544, and 550 (1956).

dent Johnson, the CSC issued a directive that further confused the question of what constitutes a sensitive position. In a letter to all departments and agencies dated November 18, 1965, CSC Chairman John W. Macy, Jr., advised that departments and agencies as a minimum must classify as "sensitive" positions whose incumbents have access to classified defense information. Sensitive positions, in turn, were to be divided into critical-sensitive and noncritical-sensitive, a practice begun by DOD. Critical-sensitive positions, according to the directive, were to include not only duties involving the development of war plans and personnel investigations—criteria fitting the Supreme Court's definition of national security in *Cole* v. *Young* in 1956—but also policy-making duties affecting the overall operations of a department or agency and "fiduciary, public contact, or other duties demanding the highest degree of public trust."[18] Underlying this new classification of sensitive positions was an expanded definition of national security that included the protection and preservation not only of the nation's military strength but also of its "economic and productive strength."[19]

The 1965 CSC directive did not clarify what kinds of duties were to be classified as noncritical-sensitive, and subsequent studies by the General Accounting Office have revealed confusion and much inconsistency in the classification of positions by different agencies. It was found that in practice agencies used this category for positions whose occupants require access to information classified CONFIDENTIAL or SECRET. Positions that involve neither access to classified information nor duties with an overall or nationwide effect on operations at times were found to have been classified nonsensitive even though they required great public trust. This included many air traffic controllers, auditors with duties for investigating, evaluating, and recommending large government programs, and guards at federal buildings where sensitive information is stored.[20] Under Section 14(a) of EO 10450, OPM is directed to "make a continuing study of the manner in which [the] order is implemented by the departments and agencies," and this oversight function is fulfilled through periodic security appraisals. These appraisals are carried out only every three to four years, however, and are limited to reviews at agency headquarters; the job descriptions available there do not fully describe the sensitivity of the duties of an agency's manifold positions. Moreover, OPM has no

18. The Macy letter is reprinted in U.S. Congress, House, Committee on Internal Security, *Hearings Regarding the Administration of the Subversive Activities Control Act of 1950 and the Federal Civilian Employee Loyalty-Security Program,* part 2, 91st-92d Cong., 1970-72, pp. 595-97.
19. *Federal Personnel Manual,* chap. 732: "Personnel Security Program," 1-1.
20. GAO, *Proposals to Resolve Longstanding Problems,* pp. 20-21.

enforcement authority and thus is unable to rectify inappropriate job classifications even when these can be discovered.

Overclassification of positions costs large sums of money—the difference in cost between an NACI required for nonsensitive positions and a background investigation for critical-sensitive positions was $960 in 1981—while underclassification may threaten important security interests. The issues of classification criteria and of the scope of personnel investigations were addressed by an interagency task force, chaired by Peter Garcia, director of OPM's Division of Personnel Investigations. The report, prepared in August 1981, proposed a new five-level system for civilian positions instead of the previous three levels in order to provide agencies with greater flexibility and to avoid improper designations and excessive investigative costs. The classification and designation of positions was to be based on an assessment of risk to the national interest associated with a position's duties and responsibilities. Most positions previously classified nonsensitive were to be placed into Level I and were to receive only an NAC. The new system would save almost $2 million, that is, about 7.3 percent of annual expenditures.[21]

The Garcia report correctly stressed the importance of including in the definition of the national interest both the nation's well-being and national security. Positions that involve responsibility for major government programs or duties concerning matters of major importance to the well-being of the nation, it argued, must be considered sensitive irrespective of whether they also entail access to classified information. If adopted, the report would also promote greater uniformity in investigative coverage and therefore would reduce the need for reinvestigation when individuals move to a new position in another agency but at the same level of sensitivity. By limiting the screening process for the great majority of positions in the civil service to an NAC, the report does away with the pretense of a loyalty check that is completely ineffective and meaningless in practice and is unnecessary in the absence of an ascertainable risk to the national interest.

We have empirical data to support the proposition that it is reasonable to confine investigations for employees in nonsensitive positions to an NAC, a check of FBI files to ascertain the existence of a criminal record. A GAO study in 1976 found that of 96,962 NACI investigations in the Chicago area, only 37 (0.04 percent) resulted in the removal of employees in nonsensitive positions. Moreover, 22 (59 percent) of these removals were the result of the NAC performed by the FBI. In other words, by relying upon an NAC rather than an NACI

21. *Federal Personnel Security Investigations Program: Interagency Study in Implementation of GAO Recommendations,* Final Report, August 1981.

the CSC would have missed 2 out of every 10,000 employees in non-sensitive positions investigated.[22] Because these employees have no duties that would enable them materially to affect agency operations, this would appear to be an acceptable risk.

A majority of federal agencies endorsed the Garcia report. The Department of Justice and the FBI expressed the fear that the new system might sacrifice security for economics.[23] DOD had withdrawn from the task force before the completion of the study because of disagreement over the use of the IBI. In late 1981 DOD ordered its own internal review of personnel security. The outcome of these various studies and the fate of their recommendations is uncertain, though some tightening up is expected.

A limitation of the loyalty provisions of the present program to sensitive positions and to those that entail access to information classified SECRET and TOP SECRET does not mean that we must ignore or slight the importance of retaining the public's trust and confidence in its government. The employment of manifestly disloyal persons at any level of the public service may undermine this trust and therefore is undesirable. Application forms should state that it is the policy of the U.S. government not to employ persons whose loyalty to the American Constitution is compromised by belief in or allegiance to a non-democratic system of government. No special machinery should be employed, however, to ascertain the loyalty of applicants for nonsensitive positions. Disloyal conduct on the job should be dealt with like any other malfeasance.

The four recommendations above for changes in the current loyalty-security program touch only upon some of the most serious shortcomings. There are other problems such as the lack of a central coordinating body for the different programs with authority to prescribe and enforce remedial action where indicated, or the difficulties that have developed in the collection of information from the general public, state law enforcement agencies, banks, and educational institutions. If Congress were to act affirmatively on the proposals made here, and before replacing EO 10450 with a new executive order, the president should establish a nonpartisan study commission, composed of members of Congress, the public, and the executive branch, in order to subject all aspects of the problems of personnel loyalty and security to a searching examination and review.

The establishment and operation of a workable loyalty-security program is the specific responsibility of the executive branch. Both the

22. GAO, *Proposals to Resolve Longstanding Problems*, pp. 36-37.
23. *Federal Personnel Security Investigations Program*, pp. B-4–B-5.

effectiveness and acceptance of such a program, however, depend to an important degree on the existence of a broadly based consensus concerning its need. The creation of such a consensus should have the same priority as the enactment and promulgation of the new program itself. There is need to demonstrate to the wider educated public that a reform of the loyalty-security program, as it is proposed here, does not constitute an attempt to take the country back to the days of McCarthyism, and that a program with a more accurate data base is needed both for the better protection of national security and in order to ensure the fair appraisal of the reliability and trustworthiness of applicants for sensitive positions in the federal government. It will be necessary to persuade Congress that without congressional willingness to spend the increased funds these changes require, especially for the creation of a qualified staff of investigators, the new program will do more harm than good. In sum, while a new program is badly needed, without backing by the informed public and Congress, cost-benefit considerations may militate against the implementation of the proposed reforms.

A NOTE ON THE BOOK

This book was edited by
Margaret Seawell and Gertrude Kaplan of the
Publications Staff of the American Enterprise Institute.
The staff also designed the cover and format, with Pat Taylor.
The text was set in Palatino, a typeface designed by Hermann Zapf.
Exspeedite Printing Service, Inc., of Silver Spring, Maryland,
set the type, and Thomson-Shore, Inc.,
of Dexter, Michigan, printed and bound the book,
using Warren's Olde Style paper.

DATE DUE